WADE
IN SCOTLAND

Van Diest pinx.   Faber fecit 1736.

The Hon.ble George Wade Esq.

Lieutenant General and Commander in Chief

of all His Maj.ties Forces, Castles, Forts and Barracks, in North Britain &c.

Sold by Faber at ÿ Golden Head in Bloomsbury Square.

[Frontispiece

WADE
IN SCOTLAND

By

J. B. Salmond

If you'd seen these roads before they were made,
You'd lift up your hands, and bless General Wade.

THE MORAY PRESS
EDINBURGH & LONDON

FIRST PUBLISHED 1934

THE MORAY PRESS
126 PRINCES STREET, EDINBURGH
39–41 PARKER STREET, KINGSWAY, LONDON

PUBLISHED BY GRANT & MURRAY LIMITED
126 PRINCES STREET, EDINBURGH

PRINTED IN SCOTLAND
BY THE RIVERSIDE PRESS LIMITED, EDINBURGH

BOUND BY
WILLIAM HUNTER & SONS, EDINBURGH

FOR MARGARET

Troop colours marked their highroad's run
  When Wade's men drove the ways.
Pennants of Ker and Harrison
  Had all the moor ablaze.
But when you and I went wandering
  Along the broken foss,
    Azaleas were the flags we met,
    With saxifrage and violet ;
    And Alpine lady's mantle set
  Her colours in the moss.

A centinel of Montague's
  With curses filled the day
When a waggon wheel had broken loose
  On a traverse north of Spey.
But when you and I went wandering
  A whaup was calling clear ;
    The ptarmigan were lazing round ;
    A cock grouse crest was blazing round,
    And a yell hind stood a-gazing round—
  The sentry of the deer.

So up the glen and o'er the ridge
  Wade's soldiers sweat and strain,
With here a traverse, there a bridge
  To build in sleet and rain.
But when you and I went wandering
  We dandered down the way,
    And the broken bridge was a resting-place,
    And the water mirrored your happy face,
    While the trout went jink in their old-time race,
  And life was holiday.

Two hundred years ago George Wade
  For war built bridge and highway.
Now Commerce finer roads has made.
  But I'll keep Wade's for my way.
For when you and I went wandering
  We knew all tumult cease.
    And birds and beasts had mind for us,
    And suns and stars were kind for us,
    And we were glad to find for us
  Wade's quiet ways of peace.

PREFACE

THIS little book is no full-dress Life of George Wade. It is an attempt to give some account of the roads he made in the Scottish Highlands, to describe their condition to-day, and to help the wayfarer to find them. The preliminary chapters tell who George Wade was, why he came to Scotland, and what he found there, and the concluding ones say something of what happened to the Field-Marshal when he finally left Scotland.

The purpose of this preface is to put on record the writer's appreciation of the courtesy, kindness and help he has met everywhere when walking Wade roads, and when seeking for information about Wade. First, he must acknowledge his obligation to the lady of the dedication, for the way she has borne with him and his King Charles' Head. There are three men to whom he is in particular debt: the late Sir Kenneth Mackenzie, Bart., for the excellent work contained in his papers delivered to the Inverness Field Club; John Mathieson, of the Royal Scottish Geographical Society, for the use of his researches, and for the way he has put his knowledge of sources at the disposal of the writer, and Francis Buist, whose unselfish provision of a mass of unpublished material can be recognized only by the thanks of friendship. To all who have walked Wade roads with him the writer's thanks are also given. To the following publishers acknowledgments are due for permission (very readily given) for quotations from their publications: Michie's *Deeside Tales* (Messrs D.

3

PREFACE

Wyllie & Son), W. Drummond Norie's *The Life and Adventures of Prince Charles Edward Stuart* (Messrs The Caxton Publishing Company, Limited), William T. Kilgour's *Lochaber in War and Peace* (Messrs Alexander Gardner), *Proceedings* (Messrs The Society of Antiquaries of Scotland). To the House Committee of the Junior United Services Club he is indebted for kind permission to consult their collection of *Wade Papers*, to the Royal Scottish Geographical Society for permission to consult their maps, and to the proprietors of *The Scots Magazine* for their readiness in permitting the reproduction of the greater amount of the writer's articles on Wade which originally appeared in that journal, and also for the use of certain blocks. He is indebted also to the following for the use of photographs:—Messrs W. Harold Thomson, H. Graeme Thomson, W. L. Weir, H. R. Cook, James Fenton, Alexander Soutter, and Messrs Valentine Ltd.; and to Messrs The Abbey Press, Fort Augustus, for the right to reproduce the sketch of the Fort.

NEWPORT, FIFE,
  May 1934.

4

CONTENTS

ILLUSTRATIONS

WADE IN SCOTLAND

CHAPTER I

PICTURE OF A ROAD-MAKER

ON Friday, 8th August 1735, a heavy coach crawled over the hill from Amulree into the Cochill valley. Some distance in front of the vehicle a detachment of Stair's dragoons rode their horses at a leisurely pace. Behind the carriage a mounted company of officers and a civilian clinked and talked. The civilian, Mr Trelawney of His Majesty's Customs, had much to say concerning the recent decisions by Parliament with regard to the petition of Robert Dalziel, late Earl of Carnwath, to Colonel Campbell of Mamore, while Colonel Guest and Colonel Duroure discussed Fort Augustus as a winter barrack, and the possibilities of the coming season's runs with the Fort George hunt at Inverness. The pace slowed considerably on the two-hundred-foot pull-up to Loch na Craige, and just at the summit, in obedience to an order from the interior, the driver brought his horses to a standstill. Out of the coach stepped a tall, burly man in the uniform of a field-officer. The horsemen had halted at a respectful distance, and their talk ceased. The big man gazed across the wide prospect that lay around him, and, as he viewed the country with his eyes, he viewed his ten years of labour for it in his mind. Away over there to the north-east rose the Beinn-na-ghloe tops. At the foot of them ran his one great road. Beyond the mist-covered Schiehallion to the north-west, his road, on which he stood, would carry him. Ten years of heart-breaking labour in a land where there was little welcome for such as he! But he had done his job, and to-day he was to inspect its crown—his great bridge across the Tay. He had hoped personally to see that bridge completed two years before, but had not succeeded. Once again in his mind he sat in his temporary quarters by his unfinished bridge on a clear October night of 1733, and let his pen pour out its annoyance to the best friend he had found in Scotland, Duncan Forbes of Culloden.

" My dear Lord Advocate," wrote the pen,[1] " I expected on my return hither to have the work at the Bridge much more advanced, than it was during a fortnight's absence and since my coming hither the weather has been so excessively bad & the floods so violent that little could be done; there is now a prospect of better, and I am pushing it on as fast as possible, the monthly charge amounting to 500m; this for all these three months past has drained me of all my money and credit; so that the Work must be laid aside in a fortnight longer; in which time I am labouring to get it as high as the Pavement and leave the Parapet Wall for another year. I shall continue here till the end of next week & if in that time your affairs shall call you to Edinburgh, I hope you will pass this way. I have had so much plague, vexation, and disappointments that Staggers my Philosiphy & believe I must have recourse to Culloden's remedy a Bumper: pray give my hearty service to him, as does all our family to you both."

A day or two later he was summoned to London, his road-work left in the (he must admit it) very capable

---

[1] Letter from Wade to the Lord Advocate, dated Taybridge, 5th October 1733 (*More Culloden Papers*, vol. iii., p. 100).

hands of William Caulfield,[1] and his military authority in the hands of Argyll. But now he was back after a long sojourn in England, and his bridge waited his coming.

The field-officer re-entered the coach, and down the hill they clattered. A draft for Colonel Hamilton's regiment at Fort Augustus climbed the bank to make way for them, their women staring in tired awe at the officers. So they came into the village of Aberfeldy. Through the ford of the Paldy burn they splashed, and came to the bridge. The dragoons had drawn up some yards from it, as did the coach. The tall man once more alighted, and mid a respectful silence His Excellency the Hon. George Wade, Esq., Commander-in-Chief of His Majesty's Forces, Castles, Forts and Barracks in North Britain, inspected every detail of what he was ever to hold as his greatest achievement —the Tay Bridge. In the midst of his inspection, he was joined by William Adam, his architect, fresh from planning a Town House for the civic fathers of Dundee.

[1] Mr William Caulfield was Wade's right-hand man in his road-construction. He was a grandson of the first Viscount Charlemont, and appears first as a subaltern in charge of road working-parties. He supervised the building of the Tay Bridge at Aberfeldy. He became Inspector of Roads in 1732, and held that position till 1767, which is presumed to be the year of his death. After Wade left Scotland, Caulfield took up residence near Inverness, at Cradlehall. He was an Irishman like Wade, and evidently enjoyed " Culloden bumpers," for his house was so named because of an after-dinner device, which was employed to hoist well-dined guests to their rooms. He acted as Quartermaster to Sir John Cope in 1745, and two years later became Deputy-Governor of Inverness Castle. Consequently he is often referred to as Governor Caulfield. He was an Irishman, and is credited with the authorship of the famous lines:

> " Had you seen these roads before they were made,
> You would lift up your hands, and bless General Wade."

In the fifth edition of Burt's *Letters*, the editor, Mr Jamieson, has a note where he states that the couplet was on an obelisk erected near Fort William. There is no record of this obelisk.

The inspection ended, officers and civilians waited for the General's opinion, but with a smile he led the way to the Green of Moness, where he was to quarter with the Highland Companies, who were in camp there, and where he had recourse to "Culloden's remedy a bumper." For there was to be a big day on the morrow.

And a big day it is for the little Highland village of Aberfeldy. Wade and his officers have been dining with the Earl of Breadalbane at Taymouth, and now in the afternoon they have ridden back to the village for the review. The Earl of Breadalbane is there, and my Lord and Lady Glenurchy. My Lord and Lady Hope chat with Lord Monzie and his lady. In fact, the parade ground is edged by all the gentry of the district. And in the square the Highland Companies, commanded by Lord Lovat and the Captain of Skipness, perform their military exercises and discharge their pieces to the entire satisfaction of the spectators and the Commander-in-Chief.

And so to a Jacobite Poet's gesture to a Whig Road-maker's work. The review is over, and through the throng rides a man on a white horse. He makes for the bridge, dismounts, and places a sheet of paper on the parapet. On the paper is inscribed a poem entitled *Tay-Bridge to the Passenger*. A reporter of that period made a copy of the verse, and it appeared as follows in the newsprints of the day:

TAY-BRIDGE TO THE PASSENGER [1]

Long has Old SCOTIA Desolation fear'd,
Pensive, 'till an auspicious Star appear'd:
But soon as the Celestial Power came down,
To smile on Labour, and on Sloth to frown;

[1] *Edinburgh Evening Courant*, 25th December 1735.

PICTURE OF A ROAD-MAKER

SCOTIA reviving, rais'd her drooping Crown:
Discord and Barrenness confess'd their Doom;
One clos'd her Feuds, and t'other op'd her Womb;
Rocks inaccessible a Passage knew,
And Men, too fond of Arms, consent to plow.

Not less surprizing was the daring Scheme,
That fix'd my station in this rapid Stream.
The North and South rejoice to see Me Stand,
Uniting in my Function, Hand in Hand,
Commerce and Concord, Life of ev'ry Land!
But . . . who could force rough Nature thus to ply,
Becalm the Torrents, and teach Rocks to fly?
What Art, what Temper, and what manly Toil,
Could smoothe the rugged Sons of Abria's Soil?
Methinks the anxious Reader's at a stand,
Not knowing, George for GEORGE (to bless the Land
Averse t'Obedience) spoke the stern Command.
And still he seems perplex'd till he is told,
That Wade was skilful, and that Wade was bold.
Thus shall his Fame, with GEORGE's glory rise
Till Sun and Moon shall tumble from the Skies.

One can conjecture that Wade took the poet off
with him to more " Culloden bumpers." The poet
was Struan Robertson, and in the mess quarters of the
Highland Companies we see these two men—repre-
sentative of the two sides in that period of Scottish
history—pledge each other—romantic Jacobite laird
and matter-of-fact Whig soldier road-maker.

These two men had been born within a couple of
years of one another, and a sketch of Struan's career,
that of a typical Jacobite, will act as a contrast to that
of Wade. Struan had been a student at St Andrews.
You can read his name there on the roll. The faded
brown ink gives it, under the date of 26th March 1688,

as " Alexander Robertsone." He forsook the University
to go Jacobiting with Dundee, was captured, but was
exchanged and allowed to join " his misfortunate
Master," at Saint-Germains, where he spent his time
cultivating bad habits, verse-writing, and the arts of
war. He did well in the first, moderately in the
second, and but poorly in the third. He wrote poems
to Albemarle, Berwick and Pitcairne, and in an ode to
the last-named these lines occur:

> " Wise was the bard who sang the sacred use
> Of the delicious grape's immortal juice,
> And found no water-drinker e'er could say,
> He shaped a verse that could survive a day."

So much for habits and verse. Of Struan's knowledge of war, Mar during the Fifteen wrote to Colonel
Hay as follows: " You must take care to please the
Elector of Strowan, as they call him. He is an old
colonel, but as he says himself, understands not much
of the trade. So he'll be ready to be advised by
Colonel Balfour and Urquhart."

On the accession of Queen Anne, in 1703, Struan
obtained a remission, and returned to his estates, but
he never even troubled to get this remission passed
through the Great Seals, so the forfeiture was never
legally repealed. He received a great welcome when
he returned to Rannoch. There he spent a peaceful
time, writing verse in the condition praised in the poem
to Pitcairne, listening to his brother's fiddle, and acting
the part of a popular landlord. So to the Fifteen, where
he marched with 500 Robertsons to Sheriffmuir, was
captured, but by the assistance of his sister escaped,
and again took refuge in Holland and France.

Struan's second return to his country was made
possible by family favour. The Earl of Portmore had

considerable influence at the Court of George I. He was a relation of Struan, and the latter's sister, Margaret, persuaded him to help her brother. It is on record that Margaret herself interviewed the King. Struan was pardoned and all his property granted to the sister, but she was " not to contract debt, or to alleviate the estate, without the special advice and consent of" a considerable number of persons. " The estate was granted to Miss Robertson and to her heirs and assignees, but revocable by His Majesty, his heirs and successors at their pleasure."

So back from France came Struan, and his actions were not those of a grateful brother. The Ochtertyre MS. states that " he took the estate into his own management, turning his sister out of possession, and treating her in a manner no less unnatural than illegal." The editor of the MS. notes : " He first imprisoned her in a small island at the head of Loch Rannoch, on which there was no house; then he sent her to the Western Isles, where she died in misery. His companions said in his defence that she was both an imperious and wretched woman, which surely did not mend matters. Even vice cannot be punished but by the magistrates. There was certainly something peculiar in the blood of that generation."

The manuscript continues : " James Moray of Abercairny told me that between 1720 and 1730 he used to go over and stay a week with Strowan, who was his relation, and always very kind to him. Nothing, he said, could be more brilliant and delightful than that gentleman's wit, or more pertinent than his remarks upon men and things. But the pleasure of his guests was diminished by the style of dissipation in which he lived. In the morning his common potation was whisky and honey; and when inclined to take what he termed a meridian, brandy and sugar were called for. These were the liquors which he generally used, not being able to afford wines, and perhaps liking spirits better."

So, up to the time of the Tay Bridge poem, Struan's life had been a bit of colourful, exciting, but rather poor verse. Wade's, on the other hand (the details will be given in the next chapter), had been a piece of fairly solid prose. The two men must have met often. What they talked about we do not know. They were both self-indulgent, and during the time of their acquaintance Struan went off to Bath to consult Dr Cheyne. Wade had lived much (and incidentally not too wisely) in Bath, and it may have been on his recommendation that the Rannoch laird set out to consult the physician there. When Struan returned, he cleared out all the women who were in attendance in his Rannoch houses.

Perhaps we see Wade and Struan at their best on that day by the Tay Bridge. Struan was at his picturesque best. Wade had just completed his best work. Each was still to live another fourteen years, during which Wade was to see Prince Charlie use his road to beat John Cope, in which he was to be outgeneralled by Lord George Murray, and at the end of which, a doddering old man, he was to die, and be buried in Westminster Abbey. Struan was to come "out" again in the Forty-five, was to be at Prestonpans, and then was to drive as far as the Wade road would take him to Loch Rannoch side, wrapped in John Cope's fur coat and riding in John Cope's carriage. While Roubiliac was busy on Wade's monument in the Abbey, Alexander Robertson died at his house of Carie, on Loch Rannoch, and 2000 persons followed the carrying-party of his clan, who bore his body all the eighteen miles from Carie to its resting-place in the churchyard of Struan.

I have begun this sketch of Wade's work in Scotland with a picture of these two men at the Tay Bridge on that August day two hundred years ago. It is a picture of Scotland not often painted. There were the gentry of Scotland prepared to accept both Struan and Wade, there was the best bridge in Scotland designed by Wade's orders by the best architect in Scotland, there were the Highland Companies, proud of their new uniforms, perfect in their drill. It was a picture of the future of Scotland—Jacobitism represented by Struan, who at the best was to make an old song, the men of the Highland Companies, the ancestors of the greatest soldiers of the finest regiments in the history of the world, and Wade, common-sense progress, realizing and allowing for the views and attitude of the Jacobite, realizing and making use of the military qualities of the Highlanders, and building and labouring in his knowledge that civilization goes along roads and over bridges. Wade made no enemies in Scotland, except in the case of Simon Fraser, and he broke Lovat when he realized it was outside that man's power to play straight with anyone. If Wade's roads destroyed the power of the chiefs, it was a power that had to be destroyed sooner or later. Wade's attitude of mind towards the Highlands of Scotland was not that it was an area that should be subdued for the benefit of England, but a place that should be policed by its own people for its own good. Let us see how he went about it.

CHAPTER II

THE MAKING OF A SOLDIER

WHEN Oliver Cromwell sailed for Ireland in 1649 he
had in his mind methods by which to reduce that
country to a complete acceptance of Roundhead
views. He began by killing as many of his enemies
as he could. He massacred some 3000 at Wexford.
What prisoners he did take were shipped as slaves to
the Barbados. Then he put into action his second
method. He first of all confiscated land over a
large area, removed the population to the wilds of
Connaught, allowed some 40,000 Irish to seek military
service in foreign parts, and then proceeded to hand
over immense tracts of land to the adventurers who
had lent his Government money, and to certain of
his soldiers in lieu of pay. One of these soldiers was
William Wade. He was a West Country Englishman,
and a major in a dragoon regiment. The land granted
to him was in West Meath and King's County, and he
settled there in 1653. He had married a Miss Stone-
street, the daughter of an English clergyman, and,
while I have found no record of their only son, Jerome,
fighting in the Protectorate army, he appears to have
settled in Killavalley, in the same county as his father.
Jerome's family consisted of three sons: William, who
became Canon of Windsor, and who was buried in
St George's Chapel, Windsor; Jerome, who succeeded
his father in Killavalley, and George, who first saw

the light in 1673. One son to the Church, one to the estate, and one to the Army was the arrangement, and George, on 26th December 1690, was gazetted ensign in the 10th Foot (the Earl of Bath's regiment). As George Wade was to finish his military career in the field against the Jacobites, it has been suggested that he began that same career against the same foe. King William, owing to the approach of winter, had been forced to raise the siege of Limerick, which was being defended in James's interest by General Sarsfield. William returned to England. But in the early spring General Ginkell utterly defeated the combined French and Irish forces at Aughrim. Sarsfield was forced to sign a treaty, and with his 10,000 Irish Jacobites departed for France. It has been suggested that Wade was at Aughrim, but there is no record of Bath's regiment being there. The regiment certainly went to Flanders in 1691, and Wade was present at the butchery of Steinkirk. His promotion was fairly rapid. In 1693 he was gazetted Lieutenant. In 1694 he became Captain-Lieutenant, and in 1695 as a Captain he commanded the grenadier company of his regiment.

After the Peace of Ryswick (1697) Wade came home with his regiment, which was under the command of Sir Bevil Branville, but returned to Flanders in 1702, when war broke out with France. The 10th Foot did particularly well in the campaign, and Wade especially distinguished himself at the siege of Liége, where with his grenadiers he stormed and carried the citadel. In March 1703 he was awarded his majority, and seven months later became Lieutenant-Colonel. He evidently saw possibilities of even quicker promotion in another theatre of war, for he volunteered for service with Lord Galway's expedition to Portugal. He sailed for that country as Adjutant-General with the brevet rank of Colonel, and on the death of the officer commanding the 33rd Foot, Wade became colonel of that regiment. He was one of the few officers to take much glory from Galway's somewhat weary campaign, and he did particularly well at the battle of Almanza in 1707.

Previously, in the retreat from Madrid, Galway himself wrote thus of Wade: "The retreat was made in such good order that the enemy, superior as they were in number, never durst venture to attack us after the warm reception 22 of their squadrons met with from two battalions under the command of Colonel Wade in the town of Villa Nova."

Wade came to England with dispatches in 1708, was promoted Brigadier-General, and returned to Spain. He arrived at Barcelona to find that General Stanhope had taken over the command in Spain from Galway and was preparing an expedition to Minorca. Wade was appointed second-in-command, and entered Port Mahon with Stanhope. The aim of the expedition was to reduce Fort St Philip, which had a garrison of 1000 men and was defended by 100 cannon. Stanhope had some 2500 troops. His first difficulty was the landing of his siege guns. The ground was very hilly and rocky, and no doubt here Wade had his first experience of temporary road-making, for Minorca, like the Highlands of Scotland, was then without roads. John Cope of Prestonpans fame was Stanhope's aide-de-camp and has left an account of how the troops "made a very good road for the cannon." The bombardment of the fort began, and the outer works were captured by Wade and his grenadiers. On the fall of the outer works the citadel surrendered.

Wade continued to add to his glories. In 1709 Charles III., the claimant to the throne of Spain, sent Wade a very complimentary letter, and gave him the rank of Major-General while serving in Spain. A year later Wade distinguished himself at the battle of Saragossa. He returned to England, and, after the peace of 1711, went on the retired list. Shortly after the accession of George I. he was promoted Major-General and given command in Ireland. There is nothing, however, to tell us that he took up this latest appointment, and we next hear of him being returned to Parliament for Hindon, in Wiltshire.

On the outbreak of the Fifteen he was dispatched to Bath in command of two regiments of dragoons. Bath was a hotbed of Jacobite plots, and Wade seems to have been very successful in their discovery. He is credited with a find of " eleven chests of fire-arms, swords, cartridges, three pieces of cannon, one mortar and molds to cast cannon, which had been buried underground." Wade further enhanced the King's opinion of him as an intelligence officer by discovering a plot hatched by the King of Sweden. Tindal (vol. ii., p. 507) gives the following account of it:

" The restless and daring Swede—many of whose past enterprises would have been deemed mad had they not, contrary to all expectations but his own, been successful—conceived a project more audacious than any that he had yet undertaken; and with insane rashness he vowed to drive George I. and the Hanoverian race from the throne of Britain, and to bring back the exiled Stewarts in the plenitude of their ancient rights and prerogatives. Certain information about this aggressive undertaking, and about the intrigues of the Swedish ambassador in London to secure the assistance of the Jacobites, had reached the British Cabinet; and the ministers resolved upon prompt measures. The conduct of Count Gyllenborg, as ambassador from Sweden at the English Court, was a flagrant violation of international law; and the Government did not scruple to resort to such proceedings against him as nothing but the enormity of his offence could have justified. On the night of the 29th of January (1716) the count's residence in London was unexpectedly surrounded by a military force under General Wade, who proceeded to carry out his secret instructions. Entering the house, and desiring to be at once conducted to the count, he found the ambassador busy among his papers.

"These the general forthwith seized upon, and summoned in a detachment of his soldiers to secure the person of the count, and to assist in the search for further documents. Madame Gyllenborg refused to unlock a cabinet, which had attracted the general's suspicions, though she assured him that it only held a quantity of linen and plate; but on his breaking it open, he discovered papers which, beyond all doubt, demonstrated the complicity of the Swedish ambassador and his Royal master in a treacherous movement against the Hanoverian dynasty, and completely justified the unceremonious and violent proceedings instituted by the Government. Among the documents was a correspondence between the count and Baron Gortz regarding 'a design to raise a rebellion in His Majesty's dominions, to be supported by a force from Sweden'!"

King George showed his appreciation of Wade's work by presenting him with the colonelcy of the 3rd Dragoon Guards, and the position of second-in-command to Sir Richard Temple against Vigo in 1719. The expedition succeeded. Vigo surrendered, and Wade added to his military laurels by capturing Pont-a-Vedra.

Wade had been very popular in Bath, and in 1722

he was elected Member of Parliament for that town, a position he held until his death. Wade's house in Bath was at 14 Abbey Churchyard. He was closely connected with Ralph Allen, who became postmaster, and later Mayor of Bath, and who married Miss Earl, Wade's natural daughter, in 1718. This lady died in 1722. Wade was a philanthropist as far as Bath was concerned. He subscribed to the building of a church known as St Michael's, headed all sorts of charity lists, and at his own expense made a passage through slums from the North Front of the Abbey, and did a great deal in the way of slum clearance. He presented at least one portrait of himself to the Corporation. It was at 14 Abbey Churchyard that Wade died. In 1769 Captain Wade, a nephew of George Wade, became Master of Ceremonies in Bath.

The Scottish Highlands at this time were very disturbed. The Disarming Act had not been successful in its functioning, and amongst other things a Memorial from Simon Fraser, Lord Lovat, on conditions in the Highlands had particularly interested the King. George looked around for a suitable man to report on the situation, and his choice fell on Wade. So in 1724 George Wade set out for Scotland on that mission which was finally to be " crowned " by the building of the Tay Bridge at Aberfeldy.

CHAPTER III

SPYING OUT THE LAND

ABOUT the year 1720 Scotland was a land of failures. The Union of the Parliaments had been a failure. As far as Scotland was concerned there had been no increase in trade. The Scottish Privy Council had been abolished. There had been interference with the Scottish Law System. Lay patronage had been restored—a violation of Treaty conditions. An attempt had been made to impose a malt tax, by which Scotland had to pay three times as heavy a duty on malt as England. Actually a Bill had been introduced into Parliament for the abolition of the Union, and it had been defeated by only four votes. The Lowlands were thoroughly discontented.

In the Highlands the situation was even more miserable. Two Jacobite risings had failed—the Fifteen because of the poor leadership of Mar; the Nineteen because of a lack of enthusiasm engendered by the failure of the Fifteen. The Disarming Act, following the Fifteen, had been shamefully unfair to the loyal clans, who handed over their arms, and were thus at the mercy of the disloyal clans, who didn't, but who imported scrap-iron weapons from Holland, sold them to the Government for good money, and retained their own sound swords and guns with which to menace their law-abiding neighbours.

So let us to Castle Dounie, and the year 1724. Here

sits Simon Fraser, Lord Lovat, biting a pen, and wondering how he can make the world, and particularly Scotland, a more profitable place for Simon Fraser, Lord Lovat. He decides to write to the King "concerning the State of the Highlands," and to tell George how Simon Fraser, Lord Lovat, can improve them with the help of the King. And here is the gist of the 1724 Memorial[1] woven by the Spider of Dounie.

Lovat, in his Memorial, explains that the people of the Highlands are entirely different from those of the Lowlands in language and dress, and " do remain to this day much less civilized." They are " very ignorant, illiterate, and in constant use of wearing arms, which are well suited to their method of using them, and very expeditious in marching from place to place." He proceeds to give details of the clan system, and the " quarrels and jealousies among the chiefs," and continues: " the use of arms in the Highlands will hardly ever be laid aside, till, by degrees, they begin to find they have nothing to do with them. And it is no wonder, that the laws establishing the succession of the crown, should be too little regarded by those who have not hitherto been used to a due compliance with any law whatsoever.

" One of the evils which furnishes the most matter of complaint at present is the continual robberies and depredations in the Highlands, and the country adjacent. The great difficulty in this matter arises from the mountainous situation of these parts, the remoteness from towns, and part thereof consisting of islands, dispersed up and down the western seas, the

---

[1] Lovat's Memorial is published in full in an appendix to the fifth edition of Burt's *Letters from a Gentleman in the North of Scotland to his Friend in London.* An interesting contemporary MS. copy is in the possession of William Mackay, Esq., of Inverness.

criminals cannot be found by any methods now practised, much less seized and brought to justice, being able to outrun those they cannot resist.

" The bad consequences of those robberies are not the only oppression which the people suffer in the loss of their cattle and other goods—but by the habitual practices of violences and illegal extractions. The Highlanders disuse all their country business, they grow averse to all notions of peace and tranquillity, they constantly practise their use of arms, they increase their numbers, by drawing many into their gang who would otherwise be good subjects, and they remain ready and proper materials for disturbing the government upon the first occasion."

Lovat proceeds to show how ineffectual the law had been in stopping these abuses, and how people were forced to pay tribute to chieftains for protection. This illegal exaction was called " Black Meall." He discusses the formation of the Highland Companies in King William's reign, and how successful these had been as police in the Highlands. " But," he continues, " after the late unnatural rebellion, the Highlanders, who had been in arms against the government, fell into their old unsettled way of living, laying aside any little industry they had formerly followed, and returned to their usual violences and robberies.

" About this time it was thought expedient to pass an Act of Parliament for disarming the Highlanders, which was without doubt, in theory, a measure very useful and desirable; but experience has shewed that it has produced this bad consequence, that those who had appeared in arms, and fought for the government, finding it their duty to obey the law, did accordingly deliver up their arms—but those lawless Highlanders who had been well provided with arms for the service of the Pretender, knowing but too well the insuperable difficulty for the government to put that Act into execution, instead of really complying with the law, they retained all their arms that were useful, and delivered up only such as were spoiled, and unfitt for service; so that, while his Majestie's enemies remained as well provided and prepared for all sorts of mischief as they were before the rebellion, his faithful subjects, who were well affected, had ventured themselves naked and defenceless, and at the mercy of their own and the government's avowed enemies.

" Upon this the plunders and robberies increased; but, upon the breaking of the independent companies in the year 1717, these robberies went on without any manner of fear or restraint, and have ever since continued to infest the country in a publick and open manner. The regular troops not being able to discover or follow them, and all the innocent people are without arms to defend themselves. Thus, then, violences are now more notorious and universal than ever, in so much, that a great part of the country has, by necessity, been brought under the scandalous contributions before mentioned (*i.e.* black mail), and the rogues have very near undone many people, out of mere resentment, for their distinguishing themselves in his Majestie's service; and others are ruined who dare refuse to comply with such illegal insolent demands.

" The method by which the country is brought under tax is this: That when the people are almost ruined by continual robberies and plunders, the leader of the band of thieves, or some friend of his, proposes, that for a sum of money to be annually paid, he will press a number of men in arms to protect such a tract of ground, or as many parishes as submit to pay the contributions. When the terms are agreed upon, he ceases to steal, and thereby the contributors are safe. If any refuse to pay, he is immediately plundered. To colour all this villany, those concerned in the robberies pay the tax with the rest, and all the neighbourhood must comply, or be undone. This is the case (among others) of the whole low country of the shyre of Ross.

"After the disarming Act was passed, and those companies were broke, there were some other measures laid down for preserving the peace of the Highlands. Barracks were built at a very great expense, and detachments were made from the regiments in the neighbourhood to garrison them, and to take post in those places which were thought most proper for the repressing these disorders; but all this had no effect. The regular troops were never used to such marches, with their usual arms and accutrements; were not able to pursue the Highlanders; their very dress was a signal to the robbers to avoid them; and the troops, who were strangers to the language, and often relieved by others, could never get any useful intelligence, nor even be sufficiently acquainted with the situation of the several parts of the country, so as to take the necessary measures for pursuing the robbers when any violence was committed."

The suggestion behind this is that Highland Companies, raised and commanded by my Lord Lovat, would make the ideal Highland Police. The Highlands were suffering from a form of American gangsterdom. Lovat, running the whole racket, would solve the problem.

Lovat proceeds to discuss the law officers. "The officers of the law, for the peace, are the Sheriffs and Justices of the Peace; and, in time of commotions, the Lieutenants and their deputies; which office, long

SIMON FRASER, LORD LOVAT

(From the Hogarth Portrait)

disused, was revived and re-established at the time of the late rebellion.

" It would seem to be highly necessary to the government, that the Sheriffs and Lord Lieutenants should be persons having credit and interest in the shyre they are to govern—they cannot otherwise have the knowledge necessary, of the gentlemen and inhabitants, for performing the duty of their office, and making it useful for the advancing of his Majestie's interest. On the contrary, such ignorance creates many mistakes in the execution of their charge tending to the interruption of justice, and rendering the people under them discontented and unwilling to act in the service of the government. In these cases, it has happened that, throw misrepresentations of the characters of the persons employed under them, deputy sheriffs have been made every way unfit for their office—ignorant, of bad reputation, and notoriously ill-affected to his Majesty.

" There are two deputies of the shyre of Inverness, both of which were actually in the late rebellion, Robert Gordon of Haughs, and John Bailie, a late servant to the Duke of Gordon during the rebellion; and both these deputies were prisoners in the hands of Lord Lovat upon that account, who has now the mortification to see and feel them triumphant over him, loading him with marks of their displeasure.

" It cannot but be a very melancholy scene for all the well-affected gentlemen and inhabitants of those parts, to find the very criminalls whom, a few years ago, they saw in arms and open rebellion in the Pretender's cause, vested with authority over them, and now acting in his Majestie's name, whom they endeavoured to destroy, and to whom alone they owe their lives."

The solution again is to give Lord Lovat the job of Lord-Lieutenant of Inverness-shire.

" The revival of the Justices of the Peace of Scotland, immediately after the Union, was then esteemed a matter of the greatest importance to the government, and interest of the protestant succession. It is, therefore, the more to be lamented, that throwout the whole north of Scotland, there is hardly any regular acting Commission of the Justice of the Peace, whereas, if the considerable gentlemen [*e.g.* Lord Lovat] were appointed, who have estates in their own county, and were all affected to his Majesty, there is no doubt but that office would be execute so as to be very useful to the government, and possibly pave the way for great improvements in the political state of the country."

George I. and his advisers read Lovat's Memorial, decided there was something in it (but recognized at the same time that there was a little too much Lovat in it), and so, on 3rd July 1724, King George instructed General Wade to proceed to the Highlands of Scotland, " narrowly to inspect the situation of the Highlanders, their manners, customs, and the state of the country in regard to the depredations said to be committed in that part of his Majesty's dominions, to make special inquiry into the allegations that the effect of the last Disarming Act had been to leave the loyal party in the Highlands naked and defenceless at the mercy of the disloyal; to report how far Lovat's Memorial was founded on fact, and whether his proposed remedies might properly be applied; and suggest to the King such other remedies as may conduce to the quiet of his Majesty's faithful subjects, and the good settlement of that part of the Kingdom."

Wade received his instructions on 3rd July 1724. He set out for Scotland on the 4th, and his report is dated 10th December of the same year. The following is a summary of that report.[1]

Wade states that there are 22,000 men in the Highlands capable of bearing arms; 10,000 are well affected to the Government, the remainder "have been engaged in Rebellion against Your Majesty, and are ready, whenever encouraged by their Superiors or Chiefs of Clans, to create new Troubles and rise in Arms in favour of the Pretender." Wade then discusses clanship, the Highlanders' method of fighting, and "black-meal." He points out that "the Clans in the Highlands, the most addicted to Rapine and Plunder, are, the Camerons on the West of the Shire of Inverness, the Mackenzies and others in the Shire of Ross who are Vassals to the late Earl of Seaforth, the M'Donells of Keppoch, the Broadalbin Men, and the M'Gregors on the Borders of Argyleshire."

He describes how cattle-thieves work, and continues:

"Those who are robbed of their Cattle (or Persons employed by them) follow them by the Tract and often recover them from the Robbers by Compounding for a certain sum of Money agreed on, but if the Pursuers are Armed and in Numbers Superior to the Thieves and happen to seize any of them, they are seldom or never prosecuted, the poorer sort being unable to support the charge of Prosecution.

"They are likewise under the Apprehension of becoming the Object of their Revenge, by having their Houses and Stacks burnt, their Cattle stolen or hockt, and their Lives at the Mercy of the Tribe or Clan to whom the Banditti belong. The Richer sort (to keep,

---

[1] This report also is printed as an appendix to the fifth edition of Burt's *Letters*. It is also published in volume one of the Spalding Club *Historical Papers, 1699-1750*. The latter also contains the 1725 "Scheme" referred to on page 38.

as they call it, good Neighbourhood) generally compound with the Chieftain of the tribe or Clan, for double Restitution, which he willingly pays to save one of his Clan from Prosecution, and this is repaid by a Contribution from the Thieves of his Clan, who never refuse the payment of their proportion to save one of their own fraternity. This Composition is seldom paid in Money, but in Cattle stolen from the opposite side of the Country to make reparation to the Person injured. . . .

" The Chiefs of some of these Tribes never fail to give Countenance and protection to those of their own clan; and tho' they are taken and committed to Prison, by the Plantiff, [who is] better satisfied than if the Criminal was Executed, since he must [be] at the Charge and Trouble of a tedious dilatory and expensive Prosecution and I was assured by one who annually attended the Assizes at Inverness for four Years past, that there had been but one person Executed there by the Lords of Justiciary and that (as I remember) for Murder, tho' that Place is the Judicature, in Criminal Cases, for the greatest part of the Highlands."

Again compare American gangsters and American law.

" There is another Practice used in the Highlands, by which the Cattle stolen are often recovered, which is, by sending Persons to that part of the Country most suspected and making an offer of a Reward (which the Highlanders call Tascal-Money) to any who will discover the Cattle and the Persons who stole them. By the temptation of the Reward and promise of Secrecy, discoveries were often made and Restitution obtained. But to put a Stop to a practice they thought an injury to the Tribe, the whole Clan of the Camerons (and others since by their example) bound themselves by Oath never to take Tascal-Money, nor to inform one against the other. This they take upon a Drawn Dirk or Dagger, which they kiss in a solemn manner, and the Penalty declared to be due to the said Oath is to be stabbed with the same Dagger. This manner of Swearing is much in practice on all other occasions, to bind themselves one to another that they may with more security exercise their Villany, which they imagine less Sinful than the Breach of that Oath, since they commit all sorts of Crimes with impunity, and are so severely punished if forsworn. An instance of this happened in December 1723, when one of the Clan of the Camerons, suspected to have taken Tascal-Money, was in the Night-time called out of his Hut from his Wife and Children and hanged up near his own Door. Another of that Tribe was, for the same Crime (as they call it), kept a month in the Stocks and afterwards privately made away with."

A perfect case of modern American " bumping-off."

Wade then discusses the Disarming Act of 1716, points out that it has failed, and states that " great Quantities of broken and useless Arms were brought from Holland and delivered up to the Persons appointed to receive the same at exorbitant prices."

Of the independent companies, he says: " The Independent Companies raised by King William not long after the Revolution reduced the Highlanders into better order than at any time they had been in since the Restauration. They were composed of the Natives of the Country, inured to the fatigue of Travelling the Mountains, lying on the Hills, wore the same Habit and spoke the same Language; but for want of being put under proper Regulations, Corruptions were introduced, and some who Commanded them, instead of bringing Criminals to Justice (as I am informed) often compounded for the Theft and for a Sum of Money set them at Liberty. They are said also to have defrauded the Government by keeping not above half their Numbers in constant Pay; which, as I humbly conceive, might be the reason Your Majesty caused them to be disbanded.

" Your Barracks were afterwards built in different parts of the Highlands, and Parties of the Regular Troops under the Command of Highland Officers, with a Company of 30 Guides (established to conduct them through the Mountains), was thought an effectual Scheme, as well to prevent the rising of the Highlanders disaffected to Your Majesty's Government, as to hinder the Depredations on your faithful Subjects. It is to be wished that during the Reign of Your Majesty and your Successors, no Insurrections may ever happen to experience whether the Barracks will effectually answer the end proposed; yet I am humbly of opinion : That if the number of Troops they are built to contain was constantly Quartered in them (whereas there is now in some but 30 Men) and proper Provisions laid in for their support during the Winter Season, they might be of some use to prevent the Insurrections of the Highlanders; Though as I humbly conceive (having seen them all) that two of the four are not built in as proper Situations as they might have been."

Wade finds that another cause of disorder in the Highlands is the want of proper Justices of the Peace. He shows an extraordinary condition of things in the case of the late Earl of Seaforth's estate. " Your Majesty's Commands requiring me to examine into the State and Condition of the late Earl of Seaforth's Estate, engaged me to go to the Castle of Brahan, his principal Seat, and other parts of the said Estate, which for the most part is Highland Coast, being 36 Miles in length and the most Mountainous part of the Highlands; The whole Island of Lewis was also a part of the said Earl's Estate. The Tennants before the late Rebellion were reputed the richest of any in the Highlands, but now are become poor by neglecting their business and applying themselves wholly to the use of Arms. The Rents continue to be levied by one, Donald Murchieson, a Servant of the late Earl's, who annually remits (or carries) the same to his Master into France.

" The Tennants when in a condition are also said to have sent him free Gifts in proportion to their several Circumstances, but are now a year and a half in Arrear of Rent. The Receipts he gives to the Tennants are, as Deputy Factor to the Commissioners of Forfeited Estates, which pretended Power in the year 1721 he extorted from the Factor appointed by the said Commissioners to Collect these Rents for the use of the Publick, whom he attacked with above 400 Arm'd Men as he was going to enter upon the said Estate; having with him a body of 30 of Your Majesty's Troops. The last year this Murchieson travell'd in a Public manner to Edinburgh to remit £800 to France for his Master's use, and remained there fourteen Days unmolested."

Then we have Wade's first mention of roads and bridges in the Highlands:

" Before I conclude this Report, I presume to observe to your Maty, the great Disadvantages Regular Troops are under when they engage with those who Inhabit Mountainous Situations. The Sevennes in France, and Catalans in Spain, have in all times been Instances of this Truth. *The Highlands of Scotland are still more impracticable, from the want of Roads and Bridges,*[1]

---

[1] The italics are mine. Here is the first mention of the question of roads and bridges for the Highlands.—J. B. S.

and from excessive Rains that almost continually fall in those parts, which by Nature and constant use become habitual to the Natives, but very difficultly supported by the Regular Troops."

The following are some of Wade's suggestions:

" That Companies of such Highlanders as are well affected to his Majesty's Government be Established, under proper Regulations and Commanded by Officers speaking the Language of the Country. . . .

" That the said Companies be employed in Disarming the Highlanders, preventing Depredations, bringing Criminals to Justice, and hinder Rebells and Attainted Persons from inhabiting that part of the Kingdom.

" That a Redoubte or Barrack be erected at Inverness, as well for preventing the Highlanders descending in the Low Country in time of Rebellion, as for the better Quartering of his Maty's Troop's, and keeping them in a Body sufficient to prevent or Subdue Insurrections.

" That in order to render the Barrack at Killihuimen (the present Fort Augustus) of more use than I conceive it to be of at present (from its being situate at too great a distance from Lake Ness) a Redoubte be built at the West End adjoining to it. . . .

" That a small Vessel with Oars and Sails be built on the Lake Ness, sufficient to carry a Party of 60 or 80 Soldiers and Provisions for the Garrison, which will be a Means to keep the Communication open between that place and Inverness, and be a safe and ready way of sending Parties to the Country bordering on the said Lake, which is Navigable for the largest Vessels. . . .

" That for the support of the Civil Government proper Persons be nominated for Sheriffs and Deputy Sheriffs in the Highland Counties, and that Justices of the Peace and Constables be Established in proper places with small Salaries allowed them for the charge they say they are (of necessity) at in seizing and sending Criminals to distant Prisons; and that Quarter Sessions be punctually kept at Killihuimen, Ruthven in Badenoch and Fort William, and if occasion should require at Bernera, near the Coast of the Isle of Skye.

" That an Act of Parliament be procured effectually to punish the Highlanders inhabiting the most un-civilized parts of the Country, who carry or conceal in their Dwellings, or other Places, Arms contrary to Law; and as the Penalty of a fine in the former Act has never been (or from their Poverty can never be) levied, it is hoped the Parliament will not Scruple to make it Felony or Transportation for the First Offence."

A fortnight after the date of this report Wade was appointed Commander of the Forces in North Britain, and he appears right away to have sent instructions from London, although he did not set out for Scotland till June 1725. In April 1725 he sent a " scheme " to the King in which he outlines how the disarming of the Highlands could be carried out, and he asks for provision of money for, among others, the following purposes:

" For building a Vessel on the Lake Ness.

" For repairing the Fortifications of Edinburgh Castle and Fort William.

" For building two New Forts and Barracks at Inverness and Killihuimen.

" For mending the Roads between the Garrisons and Barracks, for the better Communication of his Majesty's Troops.

" It is to be hoped that two years will be sufficient to put in Execution the several Services abovenamed, and that the Extraordinary Expence to the Government will not exceed Ten Thousand pounds for each Year," he concludes.

SPYING OUT THE LAND

It is quite definite that Wade took action concerning the Highland Companies before he went to Scotland. He sent full instructions to Major Duroure in an order of 15th May 1725; and, while Wade himself is packing up to come to Scotland, it will be of advantage to examine the history of the Highland Companies, and that of the forts and barracks in which they lived.

CHAPTER IV

THE BLACK WATCH AND THE BARRACKS

On the 3rd August 1667, King Charles II. issued a commission under his Great Seal to the second Earl of Atholl to raise a number of men " to be a constant guard for securing the peace in the Highlands." [1] These troops were to wage war against cattle thieves and blackmailers. In 1669 the Earl of Atholl was succeeded in the command by Sir James Campbell of Lawers, who five years later was followed by Major George Grant. The force was increased in 1677, when a committee of the Privy Council decided to form two companies, Macdonnell of Glen Garry to command one, and Campbell of Lawers the other. An adjustment was made when Menzies of Culdares and the Earl of Caithness were given command of the companies, and this Highland Watch of two companies was strengthened by a company of regular Foot Guards, who were to garrison Inverlochy. Authorities are of the opinion that it was at this time that the Highland companies were given the name of the " Black Watch," to distinguish them in their dark tartan from the " Red Soldiers," the men of the Guards' company. The Watch saw their first service when the Earl of Argyll used them in an expedition against the Macleans in

[1] For a very full and excellent account of the Highland Companies see the article " The Historic Succession of the Black Watch," by Andrew Ross, in the Marchioness of Tullibardine's *A Military History of Perthshire*.

1678. The two companies were disbanded in 1680, and two additional companies were added to the Earl of Mar's Regiment, their particular duty being to maintain peace in the Highlands. They failed to do this, and the Highlands were subsequently divided into four districts, the chief man in each district being made responsible for the peace. The Inverlochy company was re-formed and with the two companies from the Earl of Mar's Regiment (commanded by Mackenzie of Suddie and George Barclay) continued the work. Suddie was killed in a fight with the Macdonnells of Keppoch. The regular troops were withdrawn in 1688, and a temporary Watch was formed. In 1689 four independent companies were in existence, and these were increased to five in 1691. A change took place two years later, when these five independent companies were put on the pay-list of the regular regiments. There appear to be only two companies in existence in 1703. These were commanded by Alexander Campbell of Fonab and Captain William Grant. Major Duncan Mackenzie of Kincraig was given command of a new company in 1704. These companies were not with Argyll at Sheriffmuir, and they were finally disbanded in 1717.

At this time there were four permanent garrisons in the Highlands: Inverlochy (that is, Fort William), Killichiumen (later Fort Augustus), Bernera in Glenelg, and Ruthven (near Kingussie). In each of these was placed 30 Highlanders under Highland officers. Their duty was really to act as guides for regular troops who had to move in the Highlands. By Wade's instructions, six companies were raised in April 1725. The first three were commanded by Grant of Ballindalloch, Lovat, and Campbell of Lochnell. They consisted each of 114 men. The other three companies had each 71 men and were commanded by Campbell of Skipness, Campbell of Carrick and Munro of Culcairn. Stewart of Garth gives the date 1729 as that when the independent companies received pay as regular companies. Ten years later, in 1739, four additional companies were raised and the whole body was formed into a regiment of the line, known as the Earl of Crawford's Regiment of Foot, which was the direct ancestor of the Black Watch of to-day.

One of Wade's last acts in Scotland was to review these companies, in August and September 1738, at Taybridge, Fort Augustus and Ruthven. The parade state is given in his *Journal*, which is in the Library of the Junior United Service Club, as follows:

Companys	Serjeants	Drummers	Rank & File	Sick	On Party	Effective with Corporals	Wanting to Complete
Lord Lovat's . .	4	2	84	—	—	84	—
Capt. Grant's . .	4	2	77	2	2	81	3
Sir Duncan Campbell's	4	2	83	1	—	84	—
Capt. Lieut. John Campbell's . .	3	2	47	1	3	51	—
Capt. Lieut. Colin Campbell's . .	3	2	50	1	—	51	—
Capt. Lieut. Munro's .	3	2	51	—	—	51	—
Totals	21	12	392	5	5	402	3

The castle companies also were reviewed in August —300 men held Edinburgh, Stirling, Dumbarton and Blackness castles.

This short sketch of the Highland Companies may suitably be followed by some notes on the forts and barracks in the Highlands, in which these troops were stationed.

Later on in these notes the change in the defences made by Wade on such places as Edinburgh Castle will be detailed. At the moment we will deal with the development of the Highland Forts—Fort William, Fort Augustus, Fort George (Inverness), and the barracks of Ruthven and Bernera.[1]

It was Cromwell who first saw the advantages of a series of forts on the line of the Great Glen as a method of controlling the Highlanders. At Inverness he built a citadel to hold 1000 men. This citadel, called "Oliver's Fort," was built on the east bank of the Ness near the mouth. The central tower and part of the wall still remain. The building was commenced in 1652. The minister of Kirkhill wrote of it as follows [2]:

"1655.—The Citadel of Inverness is now on a great length, almost finished. It was five-cornered with bastions, with a wide trench, that an ordinary bark might sail in at full tide; the breastwork, three storeys, built all of hewn stone limed within, and a brick wall; centinel houses of stone in each corner; a sally-port to the south, leading to the town. . . . There was a thousand men in the regiment, Colonel Thomas Firth, governor.

"They fixed a garrison at Inverlochy, and carried a bark, driven upon rollers, to the Loch end of Ness, and there enlarged it into a stately frigate, to sail with provision from one end of the Loch to the other—Mr Church, governor, and Lieutenant Orton, captain of the frigate, and sixty men aboard of her, to land upon expeditions when they pleased.

"1661.—In the close of July, by an act of the

---

[1] Wade had, of course, garrisons in many other places—*e.g.* Dumbarton Castle, Blackness Castle and Inversnaid.

[2] Quoted in Carruthers' *Highland Notebook*, from the Wardlaw MS.

Parliament, an order is issued out to slight and demolish the citadels of the kingdom which were built by the English. This of Inverness had not stood ten years. . . . I was an eye-witness of the first stone that was broken of this famous citadel, as I was also witness of the foundation-stone laid, Anno 1652, in May. . . . A rare thing fell out here that was notarly known to a thousand spectators, that the Commonwealth's Arms set up about the most conspicuous gate of the Citadel, a great *thistle* growing out above it covered the whole carved work and arms, so as not a bit of it could be seen, to the admiration of all beholders!"

The citadel was never reconstructed.

Wade's fort was built on the Castle Hill. In many ways the history of the building on the Castle Hill of Inverness has been the history of the Highlands. In the twelfth century there was a castle on Castle Hill which served, as Mr Evan Barron puts it, "at once as the symbol and the seat of power of the King of Scotland in the Highlands." Scottish kings made different uses of the castle. William the Lion fixed the head of the rebel Donald Ban M'William on it, while Alexander III. had it enlarged for his residence in it. The Castle was held at different times for Edward I. and for Bruce. After Harlaw the Earl of Mar rebuilt it, and in it James I. held a parliament. In 1509 the Earl of Huntly, as keeper, strengthened it, and in 1562 Queen Mary found its gates shut against her, but, at the second time of asking, the governor opened the gates—and was hanged for his trouble.

There had been some kind of a barrack here from the time of General Mackay. The barrack, before it was reconstructed by Wade, is thus described by Burt in his *Letters*:

"The Castle stands upon a little steep Hill closely

adjoining to the Town. On the South Side, built with unhewn Stone; it was lately in Ruins, but is now completely repaired, to serve as a Part of the Citadel of Fort George, whereof the first Foundation Stone was laid in Summer, 1726, and is to consist of Barracks for six Companies.

" You will think it was a very scanty Palace, when I have told you, that before it was repaired, it consisted of only six Lodging-Rooms, the Offices below, and the Gallery above; which last being taken down, and the Rooms divided each into two, there are now twelve Apartments for Officers' Lodgings. . . .

" Before I have done with the Castle, I must acquaint you with an odd Accident that had like to have happened to it, not many Days after the abovementioned Discovery. And first I must tell you, that one End of the Building extends to the Edge of a very steep Descent to the River, and that Slope is composed of very loose Gravel.

" The Workmen had ignorantly dug away some little Part of the Foot of the Declivity, to make a Passage something wider between that and the Water. This was done in the Evening, and pretty early in the Night we were alarmed with a dreadful Noise of running about, and calling upon a great Number of Names, insomuch that I concluded the Town was on fire. This brought me suddenly to my Window and there I was informed that the Gravel was running, and followed by continual Successions; and that the Castle would be down before Morning.

" However it was prevented; for the Town Masons and Soldiers soon run up a dry Wall against the Foot of the Hill (for stones are everywhere at Hand in this Country), which furnished them with the hasty Means to prevent its Fall."

Inverness is not rid of this trouble to this day.

Wade built a very elaborate fort and barrack here. He named this building Fort George, after the King. It was held by the Royal troops till February 1746, when it was besieged by Prince Charles Edward, and the garrison surrendered. Prince Charles decided to demolish it. A French artillery sergeant, by name L'Epine, laid mines under the bastions. All exploded successfully but one. L'Epine ran forward to see what was amiss. The mine went off, and L'Epine's body was blown through the air into the river. Fort George was completely gutted.

At the request of the magistrates of Inverness, the new Fort George was built out at Ardersier Point a few years later.

Wade also, like Cromwell, had constructed a galley for use on Loch Ness. She was of about thirty tons, and carried six to eight guns, named " patteroes." " When she made her first trip she was mightily adorned with colours, and fired her guns several times, which was a strange sight to the Highlanders, who had never seen the like before."

The early name for Fort Augustus was Kilcumein (spelt in various ways), the original being Cille-chumein the Church of Cumein, one of St Columba's disciples. There is a tradition that Cromwell also had a fort at Kilcumein, but the first definite evidence that we have of a fort here is in 1716, when one was erected on the site at present occupied by the Lovat Arms Hotel. Part of the ramparts may still be seen. The barrack in this fort could hold 100 men. Wade's opinion was that this fort and barrack were too far from Loch Ness, and he began the construction of a new fort (on the site now occupied by the Monastery) in 1727. He named the new building Fort Augustus, after the man who was to become known as "The Butcher," while for some time the village round the fort was designated Wadeborough.

The fort was very strongly built, and it is on record that several years ago, when it was required to pierce a doorway through one of the bastions, " it took the mason three whole days to get through the wall." [1] The building was not actually completed till 1742. A harbour for the Highland galley was built on the south side of the fort some fifty yards up the River Tarff. In November 1745 the Frasers blockaded this fort, and in February 1746 Stapleton occupied the old barracks (on the site of the hotel), bombarded the new fort from a hill on the other side of the Oich, still known as Battery Rock, and blew up a powder magazine; whereupon the garrison surrendered. Later the commanding officer, Major Wentworth, of Guise's regiment, for this surrender was court-martialled and dismissed the service. The Highlanders did their best to destroy the fort, and, before they left it, certainly rendered it uninhabitable. An encampment, however, was made near it, and this was used as headquarters by the Duke of Cumberland in his work following Culloden. The Earl of Albemarle, who succeeded the Duke as Commander-in-Chief in Scotland, also made his headquarters at this encampment. The reconstruction of the fort was begun in 1747. In the times of peace that followed the Forty-five, the fort became a very pleasant barrack. Dr Johnson visited it and enjoyed his stay, while Mrs Grant of Laggan has left a record of the many happy days of her life there with her father, who was Barrack Master. In 1854 the cannon were taken from the fort, and no more regular soldiers were

[1] For full information about this fort see Dom Odo Blundell's *Kilcumein and Fort Augustus*.

quartered there. The Caledonian Canal had been driven through part of the grounds of the fort. In 1867 Thomas, Lord Lovat, bought the buildings, and nine years later they were handed over to the Order of St Benedict, who erected the present Monastery.

The first fort built near the site of the present town of Fort William was also an erection of Cromwellian times. It was constructed by General Monk in 1650. It stood just where the Nevis falls into Loch Linnhe, and three sides of it were guarded by water. It was made of turf and wattles, and was known as Inverlochy. In July 1690 General Hugh Mackay proceeded to strengthen this fort. He heightened its walls, increased its armament, erected barracks, and renamed it Fort William, after the King. The town he named Maryborough, after the Queen. This town in later years was known in succession as Gordonsborough, Duncansborough, and finally Fort William. It was to Mackay's fort that MacDonald of Glencoe came to take the oath of allegiance. In 1715 the Jacobites attacked the fort, but failed to take it. Wade strengthened the fort, and its garrison successfully withstood a siege by the Jacobites in 1746. The following extraordinary post-Forty-five story is told of the governor of the fort in *Lochaber in War and Peace*:

" Acting on instructions, the governor of the fort, after Culloden, was deputed to receive the submission of arms from the peasantry, and to such as came in with their muskets and claymores a free pardon was granted by the Government. In this connection, a melancholy occurrence falls to be related. One night, during the absence of the governor, a feast of conviviality was arranged by the officers, and when the Bacchanalian revelry was at its height, an orderly entered and inquired of the deputy-governor what was

48

RUINS OF RUTHVEN BARRACK

FORT GEORGE, INVERNESS

FORT AUGUSTUS

FORT WILLIAM

[page 49

to be done with three men who had just come in with their arms. ' Oh, hang them! ' was the retort, and, fearing to offend by expostulating, the messenger retired. Next morning the officer in charge was horrified to see three corpses hanging from an adjacent mill-beam, and hurriedly calling his servant he inquired what it meant. The truth was soon told, and the conscience-striken deputy could scarcely realize that his order of the previous night had in reality been literally carried out."

In 1864 the fort was dismantled and the buildings sold to a civilian. The barracks were converted into dwelling-houses. In 1889 the property was sold to the West Highland Railway Company, and the old site is intersected by the lines. The Governor's House and the entrance archway have been preserved.

There were some remains of a very early encampment on the green mound across the Spey from Kingussie on which stand the ruins of Ruthven barracks. The mound is 60 feet in height, 360 in length, and 180 wide. It is argued that the mound is artificial, and it is on record that, on sinking the well within the barrack, " planks of wood were found laid across each other at equal distances from near the surface to the base." On this mound stood the Castle of Ruthven, a stronghold of the Wolf of Badenoch. It was purchased by the Government in 1716, and a barrack was built. In 1734 Wade " erected and built in a workmanlike and substantial manner a stable for 30 Dragoons with all conveniences thereunto belonging, together with a guard-house for the security thereof." [1]

A military authority [2] thus describes the barrack:

---

[1] *King's Warrant Book XXXI.*, p. 413 : Public Record Office.
[2] Major W. Meyer-Griffiths in *Proceedings of the Society of Antiquaries of Scotland*, Fourth Series, vol. xii., pp. 25 and 28.

" Loopholed towers at the east and west corners guard the two entrance gateways, so placed that they can enfilade the south-east and north-west walls, in the centre of each of which the gateways are pierced. The walls are also loopholed, and arches all round them serve the double purpose of recessing the meurtrieres and of providing a platform for the sentry walk. The western tower, practically square, has windows and a chimney, and was probably used as a guard-room. The eastern tower, though similar, has, owing to the unsymmetrical shape of the whole building, as mentioned above, its south-east and north-east walls acute-angled. Forming the side walls of the barrack square are three-storeyed buildings, loopholed outwards, but having windows on to the square. Each block is divided into three compartments, with doors leading into the central house. As there is no trace of a governor's lodging, which in Forts George and Augustus was built over the main entrance, it is probable that one of these compartments was used for that purpose, and another utilized as officers' quarters. There are no signs now of the stone sentry-boxes so prominent on the bastions of Edinburgh Castle and Fort Augustus. They may have been battered down during the Jacobite siege. Even more striking is the absence of any sort of gun-emplacement, which goes to prove that Ruthven was essentially a barracks rather than a fort."

When Sir John Cope moved north in August 1745 he withdrew his garrison from Ruthven, leaving a certain Sergeant Molloy and twelve men in charge. Three hundred Jacobites under O'Sullivan and Dr Archibald Cameron besieged the barracks, but Molloy held out and the Highlanders retired. Molloy was gazetted Lieutenant.

During their retreat to the north, in 1746, the

Highlanders paid a return visit to Ruthven; and, on 10th February, Gordon of Glenbucket, at the head of 300 men, called upon the garrison to surrender. On this occasion the Highlanders were supported by artillery, and, seeing that resistance was useless, Molloy agreed to surrender on condition that the garrison was allowed to " carry off Bag and Baggage. This was agreed to, that Officer with his Command, viz., 12 Men, were conducted to Blair, leaving the Barracks on which the Government had bestowed vast Sums to the Highlanders, who, insensible of their own Advantages, directly blew them up." [1]

The Jacobites then marched north to Culloden. After Culloden, Ruthven was assigned as the rendez-vous of the clans, and there, receiving the order to disperse, in the Prince's own hand, the Jacobite leaders set out to seek safety where it could be found.

Bernera Barrack in Glenelg was built at the same time, and on the same plan, as Ruthven. The barrack was never of much importance and has little history attaching to it. In 1716 the Government purchased the land for the construction of this barrack from the proprietor, a MacLeod. The ground was actually the glebe of the minister of Glenelg, but in exchange he was given the farm of Buarblac.

There were other barracks in Scotland in Wade's time, but these dealt with are the important ones, in that they were the strong-points which Wade joined up with his roads.

[1] For a full account of the siege, and the subsequent career of Molloy, see Mr Francis Buist's article, " The Red Sergeant," in *The Scots Magazine* for January 1930. For much interesting information about the old Castle of Ruthven, see Macpherson's *Church and Social Life in the Highlands*.

CHAPTER V

A MATTER OF MALT

On the 29th of April 1725 the public prints of the day
tell us that the " Hon. General Wade has kiss'd his
Majestie's hand as Commander-in-Chief of Scotland,
Major-General Sybourg as Governor of Fort William,
Colonel Clayton as Governor of Inverness, and Colonel
Spottiswood as Quartermaster-General in the same
kingdom." On the 1st of June 1725 General Wade
received his warrant under the Royal Sign Manual,
and he arrived in Edinburgh fifteen days later. His
first purpose was to see that the terms of the Disarming
Act, which had been passed by Parliament at the close
of the session, were carried out. He expected trouble
and was quite prepared for it, for he had arranged that
the new Highland Companies would be in camp in
Inverness by the 1st of July. He had also four battalions
of foot there, and, as he writes in his report to the King,
dated 31st January 1726,[1] " the ship with ammunition
and ordnance stores was daily expected from London:
ovens were building at Inverness to bake ammunition
bread for the Soldiers; and 40,000 weight of biscuit
was provided for the support of the troops in their
marches into the mountains. I presume it was in a
great measure owing to these preparations, that several
of the Chiefs of the Highland Clans sent to me, even
before my departure from Edinburgh, assuring me

[1] Printed in the fifth edition of Burt's *Letters* as an appendix.

they would peaceably surrender their arms, pay a dutiful obedience to your Majesty's commands, and a punctual compliance to the Disarming Act."

But the strange thing is that Wade was not to meet trouble in the Highlands as far as the Disarming Act was concerned; but on the other hand he was to have to face a very nasty situation in the Lowlands as an outcome of the application of the malt tax. Lockhart in his *Register of Letters* gives a very good account of the position. He writes: "About the latter end of the year 1724, a resolution past the House of Commons whereby instead of the malt tax, six pence per barrell of ale was laid of additional duty on Scotland (and not extended to England) and the praemiums on grain exported from thence was taken off. As this was a plain breach of the Union, in so far as it is expressly stipulated that there shall be an equality of taxes and praemiums on trade, every Scotsman was highly enraged at it, for as it was evident that the want of the praemiums would effectually stop the exportation of grain, which would thereby become a meer drugg, no body could foresee to what hight this precedent of taxing Scotland separately from England might afterwards be extended. 'Tis impossible to express the resentment of the nation at this measure, all partys seem'd reconciled and to unite in opposing what was so pernicious to the country in general and at the same time touched every particular mans coppyhold."

As Wade himself states, "seditious Pamphlets were printed and dispersed through the country, comparing their slavery to that of the Israelites under Egyptian Bondage; that England had loaded them with burdens too heavy for them to bear; and that they were betrayed by the treacherous actings of their own Representatives. The Magistrates of Edinburgh were exclaimed against, and insulted for the zeal they had shown in suppressing and discouraging tumultuous proceedings, and requiring a due obedience to the law."

As a matter of fact, Wade's own account of the affair is as dramatic as any, and no historian, contemporary or later, has found fault with it. Wade writes:

"The inhabitants of Glasgow were still more outrageous, declaring publickly in the streets, that they would not submit to a Malt Tax, insulting the Officers of Excise, and threatening to stone them if they attempted to enter their Malt Houses; for which purpose they had piled up heaps of stones at the doors, to shew them what they might expect if they proceeded to the execution of that law. Messengers and letters were sent from Glasgow to most of the considerable towns in the Low Country, exciting them not to submit to this new imposition; but to follow the example of Glasgow, who were determined to suffer all extremities rather than comply with the payment of this insupportable Tax, as they were pleased to term it; and it was reported publickly at that time in Sterling, Perth, and Edinburgh, that the house of Daniel Campbell, Esq., Member of Parliament for Glasgow (who was represented to have been one of the Chief promoters of this law), was to be plundered on the day the Malt Tax was to take place.

"I was at this time at Edinburgh, preparing to set out for the Highlands, to proceed in the executing of Your Majesty's commands, when the Commissioners of Excise represented to me, that several of their officers had been insulted at Glasgow, and threatened with their lives, some of them forced to quit the town in disguise, and others to hide themselves in obscure places, desiring I would immediately order some of Your Majesty's troops to march thither to protect them against the rage and fury of the populace.

" I had the honour to represent to Your Majesty, before I went to Scotland, the necessity there was of having troops quartered at Glasgow, to prevent the disorders that might probably happen in that town on occasion of the malt duty, and Your Majesty was pleased to order that 5 Companies should be sent thither from Berwick, as soon as the Regiment arrived to relieve that garrison; but they being retarded in their march by the floods, occasioned by great rains that fell about that time, I gave directions for the speedy march of two of the five companies of Delerain's Regiment then quartered at Edinburgh, with orders to be aiding and assisting to the Civil Magistrate, and to protect the officers of Your Majesty's custom and excise, in the execution of their duty. These companies were commanded by Capt. Bushell, a careful and diligent officer, who marched with great expedition, and arrived at Glasgow the day following at six in the evening, being the 24th of June, the day in which, by Act of Parliament, the Malt Tax was to take place in Scotland.

" At their entrance into the town, the mob assembled in the streets, throwing stones and dirt at the soldiers, giving them reproachful language, and seemed to show great contempt for the smallness of their number (which was only an hundred and ten men), saying they were but a breakfast to them, and that they should soon repent coming thither. The guard-room was locked up, and the key taken away by the populace. The Captain bore these insults with patience, and sent for a Civil Magistrate; but none could be found to assist in dispersing the rabble, and tho' the Provost had sent billets for quartering the soldiers, the inhabitants for the most part refused to receive them into their houses. They increasing in their number, went to the house of Mr Daniel Campbell, Member of Parliament, broke it open, and began to plunder it with great rage and fury. The Captain, as soon as he had notice of it, sent to the chief magistrate, offering him his assistance in dispersing them. He answered, that he thanked him for his offer, but thought his number insufficient; so that the mob continued their outrages all that night and part of the day following: plundering and destroying the house and gardens without molestation.

"The next morning, the Provost ordered the guard to be broke open, and gave the Captain possession of it, who posted a guard there of an officer and thirty men.

"About three in the afternoon, drums were beat about the streets by women, or men in women's cloaths, as a signal to assemble the mob, who got together in greater numbers than before. The Captain, not knowing what mischief they intended, ordered all his men to repair to the guard; but the mob did not long keep their secret, for they advanced thro' the several streets that led to the guard-house, saying, Their next business was the soldiers, and crying: 'Drive the dogs out of the town; we will cut them to pieces.' The Captain, apprehensive that their first intention was to disarm him, drew out his men, and posted them in four divisions, facing the streets thro' which the mob advanced; who, as soon as they approached, without the least provocation, threw stones at the soldiers in such quantities, and of so large a size, that they wounded and bruised several of the men. The Captain spoke to them very calmly, telling them he was not come there to do them any harm, or hurt a hair of their heads, desiring them earnestly to retire, lest it should not be in his power to hinder the soldiers from firing on them. To which some of them answered, ' Return your men to the guard, and then we will retire.' The Captain, in hopes to appease them, ordered his men to face about, and return to the guard-house. Their backs were no sooner turned, but the stones showered in upon them, broke several of their bayonets and locks of their musquets, and put them into such disorder that they retired into the guard-room for shelter. The Captain, fearing they would disarm him, ordered the soldiers to advance again into the streets, and being attacked as they came out, the soldiers then fired, and killed and wounded several of them. They dispersed for some small time, but returned in greater rage and fury, and brought with them all the fire arms they could find in the town, and distributed to their men a barrel of powder belonging to the two companies, which they had seized on their first coming to attack the guard. The Provost, apprehending the rage the populace were in might occasion greater mischiefs than what had already happened, sent to Captain Bushell, desiring him, for his safety, and to avoid further bloodshed, to retire out of the town; otherways, he and all his men would probably be murdered. The Captain took his advice, and retreated to Dumbarton Castle, ten miles distant, being followed part of the way by some hundreds of the mob, which obliged him to fire some shot in the rear, to secure his retreat. There were of the town's people eight killed on the spot, besides nineteen who were wounded, two or three of which are since dead. . . .

" As soon as the account of this riot came to my knowledge, I held it absolutely necessary to take such measures as might hinder the infection's spreading to

Edinburgh and the other towns, who had been excited to follow the example of Glasgow. Orders were immediately sent to the Earl of Stair's and Colonel Campbell's dragoons, to take up their horses from grass; the first to march to the neighbourhood of Glasgow, and the latter to Edinburgh. I likewise took the liberty to order five companies of Colonel Clayton's Regiment from the garrison of Berwick, to march and join the five companies of Delorain's Regiment, who were then advanced as far as Edinburgh on their way to Glasgow, pursuant to Your Majesty's former orders. Two of the four Regiments who had received orders to march to the camp at Inverness were countermanded, and quartered at Aberdeen, Dundee, and other populous towns, who had openly declared against paying the Malt Duty. Stabling was fitted up for 100 dragoons to patrole in the suburbs of Edinburgh, and forage was with great difficulty provided for them, the farmers and others in the neighbourhood (as it were by common consent) refusing to sell their hay to the officers of the dragoons. . . .

" Having transmitted to Your Majesty's Principal Secretary of State, an account of these transactions, their excellencies the Lords Justices immediately ordered the Lord Carpenter's Regiment to march to Scotland; and highly resenting the riotous and tumultuous proceedings at Glasgow, sent me their commands to march thither with a body of Your Majesty's troops sufficient to assist the civil power in bringing the rioters to justice. Your Majesty's Advocate [1] also received their excellencies' orders to go thither in person, whose vigilance and activity might be depended on to supply the misbehaviour or want of resolution in the magistrates of that town, to inquire into their past conduct,

[1] Duncan Forbes of Culloden.

and the reason of their absenting themselves from their duty, at a time when their presence was most necessary to preserve the peace of the city. The troops assembled for this purpose were the Earl of Stair's regiment of dragoons, four troops of Colonel Campbell's dragoons, the Earl of Deloraine's regiment of foot, and the new raised Highland company commanded by Sir Duncan Campbell, with four field pieces, and eight cohorn mortars.[1] Colonel Clayton with five companies of his regiment, two troops of Campbell's dragoons, with two of the Highland companies, remained at Edinburgh, and it was thought necessary for the peace of the city, that Your Majesty's sollicitor should remain there during the absence of the Lord Advocate. The troops, being assembled in the neighbourhood of Glasgow, marched into the town on the ninth of July, without the least disturbance or opposition, the soldiers punctually observing the orders I had given them not to exasperate the inhabitants by reproaching them for having attacked and insulted the two companies who remained still at Dunbarton, lest their presence might excite the people to revenge. Quarters were provided by the magistrates, and the excise officers re-established and admitted to survey the malt-houses without clamour or complaint, but, on the contrary, treated with great civility.

"As soon as the Advocate had procured information of such of the Rioters who had not absconded from the town, he issued out warrants for apprehending them.

[1] Colonel Gardiner, who fell at Prestonpans, was commanding one of the dragoon regiments, and there is a curious note about Wade, Gardiner and Forbes in Wodrow's *Analecta* (vol. iii., p. 217: Maitland Club, Edinburgh): "The Advocat gave great offence by his open profane cursing and swearing at Glasgow, and his taking the right hand of the General (Wade), and talking in time of sermon, when in the afternoon in the church, and mocking Major Gardiner for his strictness."

They were seized by small parties of the regular troops, and committed prisoners to the town gaol, and no disorders happened thereupon.

" The Advocate proceeded afterwards to examine into the conduct of the magistrates; and, finding they had notoriously neglected their duty, thought fit likewise to committ them prisoners, and parties were ordered to guard both them and the rioters to Edinburgh.

" The peace of the town being thus established, a sufficient garrison was left there in order to preserve it; and the rest of the troops sent to quarters in towns where there might be occasion for their presence to support and protect the officers of Your Majesty's revenue.

" At my return to Edinburgh I found there had been a combination carried on by the brewers and maltsters of that town to leave off brewing, and thereby distress and enrage the people, by the scarcity of bread and beer, which such a practice would occasion; pretending that the malt tax was so heavy on them, that they could not continue their trade, but to their own loss and disadvantage; and the Magistrates of Glasgow were admitted to bail soon after their arrival. At their return to that town, they were met by great numbers of the Kirk, riding on each side their coach, and the bells ringing, with other demonstrations of joy.

" All endeavours were used at Edinburgh to spirit up the people, by giving countenance to those who had opposed the Tax. The Magistrates of Glasgow, and even the Rioters, were looked on as sufferers for the liberty of their country; but the guards being doubled, and constant patroles of dragoons kept in the streets, the populace thought it unsafe to have recourse to their old practice of riots and tumults; and the

Brewers and Maltsters chose rather to refuse the payment of the Tax, and to commit the defence of their cause to Advocates, who, they had reason to believe, were of their own sentiments.

" The troops being disposed of in all the considerable towns in the Low Country, and the Justice General on his way to Edinburgh, to be present to carry on the prosecutions against those who had acted in opposition to the law, I determined no longer to defer my journey to the Highlands, but to proceed with all possible expedition to the camp at Inverness, in order to execute Your Majesty's commands in those parts."

The finish of the affair was that the brewers yielded.

CHAPTER VI

WHO WAS EDMUND BURT?

ON the first day of August, Wade embarked from Edinburgh on His Majesty's ship *Rose*, but after four days at sea the winds were so contrary that the ship put in at Stonehaven. (Wade himself states: "I was obliged to land on the coast of Angus.") The General then proceeded overland, and on the 10th August came to the camp of the Highland Companies at Inverness. There he was met by some fifty Highland lairds, chiefly Mackenzies, who stated that they were prepared to hand over their arms peaceably. The Mackenzies requested that they might be permitted to deliver up their arms at the Castle of Brahan, but, as Wade puts it, "begged that none of the Highland Companies might be present; for, as they had always been reputed the bravest, as well as the most numerous of the Northern Clans, they thought it more consistent with their honour to resign their arms to Your Majesty's veteran troops; to which I readily consented."

Wade has left an account of the handing over of these arms. He writes: "On the twenty-fifth of August I went to the Castle of Brahan, with a detachment of two hundred of the Regular Troops, and was met there by the Chiefs of the several Clans and Tribes, who assured me they had used their utmost diligence in collecting all the arms they were possessed of, which should be brought thither on the Saturday following, pursuant to the summons they had received; and telling me they were apprehensive of insults or depredations from the neighbouring Clans of the Camerons, and others who still continued in the possession of their arms. Parties of the Highland Companies were ordered to guard the passes leading to their country; which parties continued there for their protection, till the Clans in that neighbourhood were summoned, and had surrendered their arms.

" On the day appointed, the several Clans and Tribes assembled in the adjacent villages, and marched in good order through the great avenue that leads to the Castle; and one after another laid down their arms in the Court Yard, in great quiet and decency, amounting to 784 of the several species mentioned in the Act of Parliament."

Lockhart, however, has a caustic comment on the situation. Writing to the Chevalier St George, he states concerning Donald Murchison (who was acting as factor for the exiled Seaforth): " I know from one that saw him that he has taken up and secured all the arms of value on Seaforth's estate, which he thought better than to trust them to the care and prudence of their several owners; and the other chieftains I hear have done the same."

Wade then proceeded to collect the arms of the Macdonalds, MacLeods, Chisholms, Grants, Camerons, Stewarts and others. To show the type of order sent out I print here the one to the Macintoshes, which has the further interest in that it is in the handwriting of, and is signed by, Edmund Burt, the author of the famous *Letters from a Gentleman in the North of Scotland*:

" To all of the name of Mackintosh, and their tribes and followers, in the parishes of Dunleckity, Doors,

Moy, Dallaricie, Croy, and Petty, and to all others of them inhabiting the four parishes of Badenoch—viz. Inch, Alvy, Kinghuizie, and Laggan, in the shire of Inverness, and to those in the parish of Calder, in the shire of Nairn : by George Wade, Esq., Major-General and Commander-in-Chief of all His Majesty's forces, castles, forts and barracks, in North Britain, &c. : In His Majesty's name, and in pursuance of the power and authority to me given by His Majesty under his royal sign manual, by virtue of an Act of Parliament, intitled an Act for more effectual disarming the Highlands in that part of Great Britain called Scotland, and for better securing the peace and quiet of that part of the kingdom, I do hereby strictly require and command you and every one of you on (or before) Saturday, the 18th day of this instant September, to bring or send to Inverness, all your broad-swords, targets, poynards, whinzars, or durks, side pistol or side pistols, guns, or any other warlike weapons, and then and there to deliver up to me, or the Governor of the said town, as is above mentioned, all and singular your arms and warlike weapons for the use of His Majesty, his heirs and successors, and to be disposed of in such manner as His Majesty, his heirs and successors, shall appoint ; and by so doing you will avoid the pains and penalties by the said Act directed to be inflicted on all such person or persons who shall presume to refuse or neglect to pay a due obedience to the same.

"Given under my hand and seal at Inverness this 6th day of September 1725.

"*(Signed)* GEORGE WADE.
"*(Signed)* EDMUND BURT."

Burt's exact position in Scotland has never been definitely ascertained. Jamieson, in his edition of the

WHO WAS EDMUND BURT?

Letters, puts him down as " Captain Burt, an Officer of Engineers, who, about 1730, was sent into Scotland as a contractor." But the corps of engineers had no military rank till 1757, and here we have Burt in Scotland signing an order at Inverness in 1725. The only thing that suggests that Burt might have been a civil engineer is his obituary notice in *The Scots Magazine*, where it states: " Feb. 4, 1755.—At London, Edmund Burt, Esq., late agent to General Wade, chief surveyor during the making of roads through the Highlands, and author of the Letters concerning Scotland." " Chief surveyor " here might refer to Wade. Because Burt mentions the roads in his letters that is no reason for connecting him with them. It seems perfectly obvious that Burt had some kind of a civilian revenue job at Inverness. The late Sir Kenneth S. MacKenzie's views about Burt's position appear to be absolutely sound. Sir Kenneth writes[1]: " Burt's real employment at Inverness was to collect the rents of an unsold residue of the estates which had been forfeited after the Rebellion of 1715. The powers of the Commissioners on these estates expired on the 25th March 1725. They had then sold most of the forfeited properties, but there remained on their hands, together with some trifling pendicles, two of the principal estates to which, in their final report, dated 17th April 1725, they thus refer:

" ' Your Commissioners and Trustees have not sold the estate of John Grant, late of Glenmoriston, for that they could not get into possession thereof so as to ascertain the true yearly value: their Surveyor having returned the same to be about £57, and their factor upwards of £150 per annum. . . . Neither have they sold the estates of William, late Earl of Seaforth, not

---

[1] *Transactions of the Inverness Scientific Society and Field Club*, vol. v., pp. 154-155.

having been able to obtain possession, and consequently to give the same to a purchaser.'

" With the expiry of the Commission these estates fell to be administered by the Treasury, and in the Treasury Minute-Book, under dates the 26th May and the 7th June 1725, there are entries of Edmund Burt's appointment to be ' receiver and collector of the unsold forfeited estates in Scotland at £400 per annum for himself, deputys and charges, to commence from Midsummer next, 1725.' His commission under the Privy Seal is recorded at length in the *Treasury Entry-Book for North Britain* (vol. 7, p. 349), and the rentals he has to account for are there specified. After the disarming of the Mackenzies in the autumn of this year, General Wade, writing from Brahan Castle on the 31st of August to the Duke of Newcastle (Dom. S.P.—Scotland), says:—' Mr Burt, the gentleman appointed the receiver of the rents of this estate, is here with me, and is promised a punctual payment of them for the use of the public.' Wade does not seem to have trusted entirely to this promise, for among the orders in the MSS. in the British Museum is one of the 28th September following, instructing officers commanding troops and garrisons in the Highlands ' upon due application made by Mr Burt, or by any of his substitutes, forthwith to send with him such a party of men as shall be thought necessary to assist in collecting the rents of the estate, formerly the Seaforth's.' The Glenmoriston estate was sold in 1730, and that of the Seaforths in 1741, both being purchased for the representatives of the old families. With this, Burt's employment, of course, came to an end, but he may have been compensated by some other office. In the MS. letter-book of Mr Duncan Grant, merchant, Inverness—lately in the possession of the deceased

WHO WAS EDMUND BURT?

Mr John Noble,[1] bookseller—there is a letter, written in 1745, by Mr Grant to Edmund Burt, then in London, saying that he draws on him for £92, 10s. 3d. at ten days after sight, on account of coals and candles supplied to the garrison of Fort George, Inverness, for the twelve months ending on the 17th June; and as it was the Barrack Master's province to supply these articles Edmund Burt probably then held this appointment. While he was at Inverness he seems to have been one of the Justices of the Peace whose appointment Wade had recommended, and the *Transactions of the Inverness Field Club* show (vol. 2, p. 83) that he shared their unpopularity. He was employed by Wade in 1726 'to state and adjust all accounts whatever relating to the Highland Galley' on Loch Ness, but the charge of the roads was committed to Roger de Bize, who had been appointed baggage-master and inspector of roads in December 1725, and whose requirements in the way of working parties for the roads the commanding officers of regiments in the Highlands were in the following year directed to supply. Burt's engagements gave him every opportunity, therefore, of observing the population of the Highlands north of Inverness, but did not take him into the regions where the roads were being made except on his occasional visits to the South."

---

[1] In his *Miscellanea Invernessiana*, p. 20, Noble writes : " The author of the *Letters from a Gentleman in the North of Scotland to a Friend in London, containing a description of a capital town (Inverness) in that Northern Country*, etc., 2 vols., 1754, was one Burt, an understrapper commissary, who, as is natural to such people, was, in his own opinion, a man of great consequence. Major Hepburn of Aldercro's regiment mentioned at Madras an anecdote of Burt, which I think happened at Inverness. Burt, giving himself some consequential airs, said he represented His Majesty. Upon which a dry Scot replied, 'Hoot, mon ! you represent His Majesty !—He, God bless him, is muckle better represented on a Bawbee.' "

Just how much Burt was disliked appears in the following letter from an Inverness magistrate to the Lord Advocate:

" As we have at all times out of our affection to his Magesti's person and Government endeavoured to cultivate a friendship with the troops quartered amongst us, It is with the greatest reluctance that we declare it impossible for us to bear with the haughty, keen and unsupportable government of these military and stranger judges set over us. We mean Coll Clayton and Mr Burt Justices of the Peace and Major Ormisby of Genrl Whitney's regiment. It is not possible for us to give your Loyt. due account of the many insults and indignities offered us, we have no better terms from Coll Clayton than ' trucklers.'

" It is common for the last two to say in the coffee-house that we are corrupt and partiall Judges—that we have neither law nor Justice in our country—Dam our Laws.

" They, and Justices of Peace above named, will lay all matters before them and shew up the English law, and they will support and execute their sentences by their military force.

" If at any time we complain to the Governor of the injustice done the inhabitants by the soldiers, we meet with haughtiness and flashes of passion, instead of redress; we are publickly certified every day almost by Major Ormisby That if he see but three town's people in a tuilzee (or a mob as he calls it), That, by God, he will Disperse them that moment by Bullot, That he'l let us know that he is not oblidged to read a proclamation, or wait dispersing of a mob one minute, and to convince us that he is in earnest, the oyr day, when we were going by the Guardroom with a buriell, the Guard was turned out and ordered to charge their peices with Ball, and put fresh powder in their pans, which was at our sight execute; and as we know not how farr a man of Mr Ormisby's complexion might mistake a Buriell or some such occasion for a mob, we represented to the Governor that we did not understand such management, who told us in derision that what the Major did was to do us honour, and all the excuse for this threat to shoot us is that we only fined in £90 Scots a fellow who exchanged some words (and a blow as appears by the testimony of our witness) with a serjeant, whereas the Governor, Mr Burt, and Mr Ormisby would have him whipt by the hangman within ane inch of his life, which is a punishment your Loyt. has told us many times we could not inflict for such a crime. However, seeing Mr Clayton was not humor'd in this matter, and by verball complaint in court he tells us that if we are troublesome he will very soon take all power out of our hands.

" My Lord, if such treatment as we meet with dayly be the effect of lodging a judicative power in the hands of strangers and military, we cannot longer boast of being free-born subjects, but must acknowledge ourselves slaves to the pride and passion of such as profess not only ane ignorance of our law, but ane utter abhorrence of all our countrymen without distinguishing betwixt such as wish well to the present constitution or not. And, therefore, as these are not our sentiments alone but of every individual of the town, we do expect from your Lordship a substantial immediate relief, and such as will free us for the future from the Tyrannie of those passionate men, or otherways we might make a surrender of our effects to those (military men) who thirst so much for civil power.

" INVERNESS, 21st *January* 1726.
" *To the* LORD ADVOCATE."

During the period that Wade was completing the disarming of the Highlanders he was also attending to the drilling of the Highland Companies, and now he sent them out on their police duties. Lovat's company was to guard all the passes from Skye to Inverness, Grant's those from Inverness to Dunkeld, and Campbell's those from Dunkeld to Lorne. The three remaining companies were posted at Fort William, Killichiumen and Ruthven. Wade then set out to disarm the clans at Braemar, Perth, Atholl, Breadalbane, Menteith, Stirling and Dumbarton. Altogether in 1725 Wade collected 2685 arms, which he dumped in Edinburgh Castle, Fort William and Bernera. At the same time he issued 230 licences to carry arms to "the Forresters, Drovers and Dealers in Cattle, and other merchandize, belonging to the several clans who have surrendered their arms, which are to remain in force for two years, provided they behave themselves during that time as faithful subjects to Your Majesty, and peaceably towards their neighbours. The names of the persons empowered to wear arms by these licences are entered in a book, as also the names of the Gentlemen by whom they were recommended, and who have promised to be answerable for their good behaviour."

Here is the form of a Licence for Carrying Arms issued by Wade:

"In virtue of the power and authority to me given by His Majesty, I do hereby permit and authorize you (A.B.), drover or Dealer in Cattle, or other Merchandize, to keep wear and carry with you, upon any your lawful occasions, from the date hereof, to the first of August, 1727, the following weapons: viz. a gun, sword and pistol; ye behaving in all that time as a faithful subject of his Majesty, and carrying yourself peaceably and quietly towards the people of the country. Dated at Inverness, 18th August 1725.

"*(Signed)* GEORGE WADE."

By the end of 1725 Wade is able to state that "the imposition commonly called black-meal is now no longer paid by the inhabitants bordering on the Highlands; and robberies and depredations, formerly complained of, are less frequently attempted than has been known for many years past, there having been but one single instance where cattle have been stolen without being recovered and returned to their proper owners."

In fact, in the later months of 1725, Wade had put in a tremendous amount of work. He had built and launched his galley on Loch Ness. It could be propelled by oars or sails, and could carry fifty to sixty soldiers. He had made nine miles of his road between Killichiumen[1] and Fort William. He had been held up in his work of fort and barrack building at Inverness and Killichiumen because he could get no contractors in the Highlands, and he had to send to Norway for timber.

Wade attributes much of his success in this first year of his work to the fact that the King had granted him power to receive the submissions of persons attainted of high treason. "It was no sooner known," he writes, "that Your Majesty had empowered me to receive the Submissions of those who repented of their crimes, and were willing and desirous for the future to live peaceably under Your mild and moderate government, but applications were made to me from several of them to intercede with Your Majesty on their behalf declaring their readiness to abandon the Pretender's party, and to pay a dutiful obedience to Your Majesty; to which I answered that I should be ready to intercede in

[1] Wade's spelling.

their favour when I was farther convinced of the sincerity of their promises; that it would soon come to their turn to be summoned to bring in their arms; and, when they had paid that first mark of their obedience, by peaceably surrendering them, I should thereby be better justified in receiving their submissions and in recommending them to Your Majesty's mercy and clemency.

" As soon as the respective clans had delivered up their arms, several of these attainted persons came to me at different times and places to render their submissions to Your Majesty. They laid down their swords on the ground, expressed their sorrow and concern for having made use of them in opposition to Your Majesty; and promised a peaceful and dutiful obedience for the remaining part of their lives. They afterwards sent me their several letters of submission, copies of which I transmitted to Your Majesty's Principal Secretary of State.

" When the news came that Your Majesty was graciously pleased to accept their submission, and had given the proper orders for preparing their pardons, it was received with great joy and satisfaction throughout the Highlands, which occasioned the Jacobites of Edinburgh to say (by way of reproach) that I had not only defrauded the Highlanders of their arms, but had also debauched them from their loyalty and allegiance."

Among the petitions sent in to Wade one of the most illuminating is from that too much respected cateran Rob Roy. Here it is:

15th Sept. 1725

From ROBERT CAMPBELL, *alias* M'GREGOR, commonly called ROB ROY

SIR,

    The great humanity with which you have constantly acted in the discharge of the trust reposed in

you, and your having ever made use of the great powers
with which you are vested, as the means of doing good
and charitable offices, to such as ye found proper subjects of compassion, will, I hope, excuse my importunity
in endeavouring to approve myself not absolutely un-
worthy of that mercy and favour your Excellency has
so generously procured from His Majesty for others in
my unfortunate circumstances. I am very sensible
nothing can be alledged sufficient to excuse so great a
crime as I have been guilty of, that of Rebellion; but
I humbly beg leave to lay before your Excellency some
particulars in the circumstances of my guilt, which I
hope will extenuate it in some measure. It was my
misfortune, at the time the Rebellion broke out, to be
lyable to legal diligence and caption, at the Duke of
Montrose's instance, for debt alledged due to him. To
avoid being flung into prison, as I must certainly have
been, had I followed my real inclinations in joining the
King's Troops at Stirling, I was forced to take party
with the adherents of the Pretender; for, the country
being all in arms, it was neither safe, nor indeed possible,
for me to stand neuter. I should not, however, plead
my being forced into that unnatural Rebellion against
His Majesty King George, if I could not at the same
time assure your Excellency, that I not only avoided
acting offensively against his Majesty's forces upon all
occasions, but on the contrary, sent his Grace the Duke
of Atholl all the intelligence I could from time to time,
of the strength and situation of the Rebels; which I
hope his Grace will do me the justice to acknowledge.
As to the debt to the Duke of Montrose, I have discharged it to the utmost farthing. I beg your Excellency
would be persuaded, that, had it been in my power,
as it was in my inclination, I should always have acted
for the service of His Majesty King George; and that

one reason of my begging the favour of your inter-
cession with His Majesty for the pardon of my life is,
the earnest desire I have to employ it in his service,
whose goodness, justice, and humanity are so conspicuous to all mankind. I am, with all duty and
respect, your Excellency's most, &c.,

"ROBERT CAMPBELL."

Wade's general clean-up of Scotland in 1725 had
cost only £2000, and he set himself down an ambitious
programme for the following year. He was to build his
forts and barracks at Inverness and Killichiumen. At
the latter place he was to build a harbour for his galley.
He further suggests to the King that barracks be placed
in the large towns, and that a man-of-war be sent to
cruise on the north-west coast " to prevent as much as
possible the correspondence that has for many years
past carried on between the emissaries of the Pretender
and the Highlanders."

CHAPTER VII

ROAD-MAKING AT LAST

In a letter to Lord Townshend, written from Killi-chiumen, and dated 16th September 1726, Wade writes:

"I have inspected the new road between this place and Fort William, and ordered it to be enlarged and carried on for wheel-carriages over the mountains on the south side of Lake Ness as far as the town of Inverness, so that before midsummer next there will be a good coach road from that place to Fort William, which before was not passable on horseback in many places. The work is carried on by the Military with less expense and difficulty than I at first imagined it could be performed; and the Highlanders, from the ease and conveniency of transporting their merchandise, begin to approve and applaud what they at first repined and submitted to with reluctancy."

Early in 1727 he writes again to Townshend, asking for further money for this same road, while he makes the suggestion that the road "may be continued to Perth at a very moderate expense by the regiments quartered in these parts." On 11th June of this year George I. died, but Wade's commission was continued by George II., and it is to this sovereign that the Lieutenant-General (his promotion is dated 7th March) sends a lengthy report [1] at the beginning of 1728.

---

[1] This report is published in the Spalding Club *Historical Papers, 1699-1750*, vol. i.

Wade had been keeping his eye on Jacobite plotters, and, with the threat of a Spanish landing on the West Coast before him, he had strengthened the Highland Companies, and had cleared them of such men as were plainly of the Jacobite persuasion. The Companies could now be formed into a battalion 525 strong. Wade also increased the strength of his garrisons in the castles of Edinburgh, Stirling and Dumbarton, and made a further search for weapons in the Highlands, " but none were discovered except about twenty muskets that had been hid in a cave ever since the Highlands were disarmed in 1725, and those grown so rusty that they were entirely unfit for service."

Wade had a sort of fatherly talk with such chiefs as he knew had been approached by the Jacobite agents, " upon which they Answer'd, that they had suffered sufficiently for their past Folly, but were now determined to live peaceably and quietly, and hoped by their future good behaviour to deserve Your Majesty's Favour and Protection." Wade arrested Stirling of Keir, but failed to seize Brigadier Macintosh. The General further reports how successful the results of disarmament in the Highlands have been, and then he goes on to detail his progress with regard to road-making and fortification :

" I presume further to Report to Your Maty, That the great Road of Communication extending from the East to the West Sea, through the middle of the Highlands, has been successfully carried on upon the South side of the Lakes from Inverness to Fort William, being near 60 miles in length, and is made practicable for the March of Artillery or other Wheel Carriage, as may appear from my having travell'd to that Garrison the last Summer in a coach and Six Horses to the great Wonder of the Inhabitants, who, before this Road was made, could not pass on Horseback without Danger and Difficulty. This work was very troublesome from the Interposition of Rocks, Bogs and Mountains; Yet was perform'd by Your Maty's Troops Quarter'd in those parts without Assistance from the People of the Country. The Non-Commission Officers and Soldiers are allow'd double pay during the time they are employed in this Service; And if it is Your Maty's pleasure to continue the same allowance out of the contingencies of the Army as was granted by his late Maty for the two preceeding years, with some Addition for erecting Stone Bridges, where they are wanting, a Military Way may be made through the Mountains from Inverness Southwards as far as Perth, which will open a short and speedy Communication with the Troops Quarter'd in the Low Country, Contribute to civilize the Highlanders, and in my humble opinion will prove the most effectual Means to continue them in a due Obedience to Your Maty's Government.

" In regard to the Fortifications in Scotland, I humbly presume to Represent to your Maty; That till the last year, nothing had been effectually done to Secure them from the danger of a surprize, to which they have been exposed for many years past; And particularly the Castle of Edinburgh, which, I humbly conceive, is a place of the greatest Importance to the Safety of that Part of your Maty's Dominions.

" The Parapet Walls of this Castle were so ruinous that the Soldiers after the shutting the Gates had found a Way to ascend and descend to and from the Town of Edinburgh whenever they thought fit.

" Upon viewing this Defect the last Spring, Four Soldiers (some of them with their Arms on their shoulders) were ordered for the Experiment to try if they could ascend the Rock and get over the Wall, which they perform'd with such Dexterity; That from the Common Road, they mounted into the Castle in less than five minutes.

" The Castle of Dumbarton had lain exposed in the same manner for some time passed, by the fall of a Considerable part of the Wall on the North side, but upon the Representation I made of this to the present Mastr Genl of your Maty's Ordnance Orders were immediately given for repairing these Defects, which was accordingly executed before I left Scotland.

" The new Fortification erecting at Inverness, call'd after Your Maty's name, Fort George, is situate on a Hill on the South side of the River Ness, near the place where it falls into the East Sea, as Fort William does on the Western Ocean. The Lake Ness, and other Lakes extending almost from one of these Forts to the other in a Streight line, through the middle of the Highlands. It is built within half Musket Shot of the Bridge of Inverness and Consequently commands that Pass which is the only communication between the North and South Highlands for the Space of near 30 English Miles as far as Killihinmen, and is therefore in my humble opinion a place of Importance for preventing the Northern Highlanders from descending into the Low Country in times of Rebellion. This fortification is irregular as are all the other Castles and Forts in Scotland, which are generally built upon Eminencies, incapable by their Situation to admit of regular Works. It is large enough to contain a Barrack for 300 Men, that number being more than Sufficient for the defence of a place which in all probability will never be attack'd by Artillery. The repairs of the Old Castle, designed to serve as Lodgings for the Officers of the Garrison, were compleated in Novemr last; And the New Works were begun the last Summer; And if continued may be capable of receiving a Garrison in two years.

"The Fort and Barrack proposed to be built at Killihinmen near the West End of the Lake Ness is not yet begun, but Materials are providing to go on with the Work, next Spring, as soon as the Season of the Year will admit. This Place being in the Center of the Highlands, equally distant from Fort George and Fort William, will, I humbly conceive, be a proper Situation for the Residence of a Governour, who, if it is Your Maty's Pleasure, may have the Chief Command, not only of the two Forts above mention'd, but of all the Barracks and Independant Companys in the Highlands, by which he will be enabled speedily to assemble a Body of 1000 Men, to March to any part of that Country for preventing or suppressing Insurrections; To inspect into everything that may regard Your Maty's Service in that remote part of Your Maty's Kingdom of Great Britain; To curb the Insolence of such of the Inhabitants, who, depending on the Strength of their inaccessible Mountains, shall presume to Rebell against their Sovereign, or insult Your Maty's Peaceable Subjects in the Low Country, and continue to disregard all Laws both Human and Divine."

In an interesting article in the *Proceedings of the Society of Antiquaries of Scotland*, Fourth Series, vol. xi., page 17, Sir R. Anderson reproduces several plans of Edinburgh Castle, and a comparison of the 1725 plan with the 1735 one shows the improvements made by Wade. Of these plans the author writes thus in the article:

"I now show two plans at present in the collection of plans belonging to the Office of Works. The first one is dated 1725. Its interest is that it shows the original arrangement of the walls, &c., at the postern-gate on the west side, and a pathway is clearly indicated leading up to it from the bottom of the rock. I have had this path examined, and there are distinct evidences of it still remaining. The first notice of this gate goes back as far as 1093. Queen Margaret died in the Castle on 16th November 1093, when Donald the Fairhaired, the younger brother of Malcolm III., had himself proclaimed king and invested the Castle with the hope of capturing the children of Queen Margaret, putting them to death, and securing the crown to himself. Apparently he knew nothing of this postern-gate on the west side, so he confined his attention to the access to the Castle from the town or east side. The children escaped by this postern-gate, and fled to England, and the body of the dead Queen was conveyed to Dunfermline and buried there. It was also at this postern-gate that the celebrated interview took place, on 18th March 1689, between Viscount Dundee and the Duke of Gordon.

" The other plan is dated 1735, ten years later than the one just described. It shows very distinctly the arrangements at the sally-port. The original wall projected considerably and was rounded like a tower, forming a very deep re-entering angle, and in the recess thus formed was the actual postern-gate of the Castle. In Slezer's view of Edinburgh Castle from the west the arrangement indicated on the plan I have just described is clearly shown. It was thus sufficiently screened from outside observation and well protected against any attempt to surprise and force an entrance. All these arrangements were done away with about 1735, as I find that on another plan relating to this part of the Castle it is stated that the alterations here were carried out by instructions from General Wade, who was in Scotland from 1726-1738. At the bottom of the rock close to the path in the gardens lies a large mass of rubble masonry. This had become detached when making the alterations above, and rolled down until it came to rest in the position in which it had been lying since about 1735. An entirely new wall was rebuilt with a postern-gate, and up till within a few years ago a small guard-house existed on the inside. This postern-gate is now built up on the inside, but is shown as a gate from the outside. Above this gate has been placed a tablet with the following inscription on it:

At this Postern John Graham of Claverhouse, Viscount Dundee, held a final Conference with the Duke of Gordon, Governor of Edinburgh Castle, on quitting the Convention of Estates, 18th March 1689.

"This interesting and very appropriate inscription is true as to the fact that an interview did take place, but not true that it took place at this particular gate, as I have just shown that the whole of this part of the fortifications had been pulled down and rebuilt as it now exists. The interview, therefore, could not have taken place here, but at the old sally-port."

CHAPTER VIII

YEAR IN, YEAR OUT

THERE has been much debate about which military roads were actually constructed by Wade, and it may be to advantage to consider his work in Scotland year by year, with special reference to the *King's Warrant Books* and Treasury documents of the period. A study of the newspapers of the time is helpful, for in these sheets can be found the dates and details concerning Wade's personal movements. Wade does not appear as a rule to have wintered in Scotland.

1726

This year Wade arrived in Edinburgh about the beginning of July. *The Caledonian Mercury* gives a detailed account how, on 12th July, " the Royal and Most Honourable Company of Archers march'd from the Parliament Close thro' this City, to the Links of Leith, with a Grace and Appearance truly great and martial, and far beyond what ye call military, to the entire Satisfaction of all true lovers of the Country. And since a Narration of what was so agreeably diverting to the Spectators cannot but give some Entertainment to those who had not the good Fortune to be on the Spot, we have thought proper to publish such an Account thereof as may be expected in a Newspaper.

    1. The Procession was opened by a Detachment of the City Guard, commanded by an Officer;

followed by the Retinues and Equipage of
Noble Lords, &c., after which came the Musick
of all Sorts, alternately answered by the Drums
and Highland Pipers posted in several Divisions.

2. The Rt. Honourable the Earl of Crawford,
   Major, on horseback.

3. The first Division, led on by the Rt. Honourable
   the Earl of Wemyss, Lieutenant - Colonel
   (in the Absence of his Grace the Duke of
   Hamilton, Captain General), followed by
   David Drummond, Esq., preses.

4. The 2nd Division commanded by the Laird of
   Glenbervie and the Rt. Honourable the Earl
   of Strathmore.

5. The 3rd Division, by the Lord Rollo.

6. The 4th Division, by the Earl of Aboyne.

7. The 5th Division, the Royal Standart, carried
   by the Laird of Marchiston, and supported by
   the Lairds of Keith and Roslin.

8. The 6th Division, by the Earl of Kintore.

9. The 7th Division, by Sir Archibald Primrose.

10. The 8th Division, by the Lord Bruce.

11. The 9th Division, by the Lord Ramsay.

12. The 10th Division, by the Earl of Cassils.

13. The 11th Division, by Sir John Nisbet of Dean,
    which last Division was followed up by the
    Rt. Honourable the Earl of Wigton. The
    Flanks being guarded by the Honourable
    Sir Robert Baird of Sauchtonhall and Mark
    Carss of Cockpen, Esq., Adjutants-General on
    Horseback.

" The several Divisions consisted of near 200 Persons
of Quality and Distinction, &c., all in their proper
rich Habits, with blue Bonnets and St Andrew in Front,
and Cockades of White and Green.

" The Officers saluted in Canongate his Excellency General Wade, who very civilly returned the Compliment. Two Captains Guards, then on Duty in Canongate, received the Noble Corps, with all imagined Respect and Deference; as did the Officer on Guard at Leith.

" There were many Thousand Spectators in the Links to see the Cavalcade, which was concluded with Shooting for the City Arrow, and won by the Mars-like Hero the Earl of Wigton. After which the Noble Band march'd into Leith to Dinner."

How Sir Walter Scott would have enjoyed this performance!

Wade seems to have spent most of July in Edinburgh, reviewing various regiments. He proceeded to the Highlands in the beginning of August, and returned to Edinburgh in the middle of October, where he put in some considerable time in examining the fortifications of the castle, and in making arrangements for the building of barracks in the Canongate. He was back in London by the end of November, and was busy with his duties there as Member of Parliament for Bath.

1727

Wade appears to have been in the Highlands about 20th July, and the Edinburgh news-sheets of 1st August stated:

" This Week a great many Shovels, Pick-axes, Wheelbarrows, &c., are to be sent hence from Killiwhimen, in Lochaber, where General Wade is about to erect a Town (to be called Wadesburgh) which is to have a Square of Barracks at each End, and to be otherwise fortified. The new Works in the Castle, which were begun when his Excellency was here, are continued; Three or four Batteries are building in the Places that seem to be weakest, where also new Guardhouses are to be set up; the Entry to the Castle is to be demolished, and a new one to go in a straight Line from the Castle-hill to the Centre of the Garison, &c."

Wade was back in Edinburgh by the beginning of September, where he reviewed Grove's regiment on Leith Links. At this review several of the soldiers' pieces burst and many men were wounded. Wade left for London on the following day.

1728

In this year Wade began his great road from Inverness to Dunkeld. On 20th July he writes from Blair in Atholl to Pelham:

"I am now with all possible diligence carrying on the new road for wheel-carriages between Dunkeld and Inverness, of about 80 English measured miles in length, and, that no time may be lost in a work so essential for His Majesty's service, I have employed 300 men on different parts of this road that the work may be done during the favourable season of the year."

On 27th August *The Caledonian Mercury* states:

"By Letters from Inverlochy of the 16th current we learn that his Excellency General Wade has been viewing the lead Mine belonging to Alexander Murray, Esq., of Stanhope, in which he is an Adventurer and whereof they give the following Account; That among the several Edge Veins already discovered, there is one lately found, that in appearance exceeds any Thing that hitherto has been seen in Great Britain; It is already discovered about 2 English Miles in Length, carrying for most part within a Fathom of the Surface of the Ground very good Ore of an extraordinary breadth, in many Places, particularly in one, where when the same was measured it was found to be 13 Foot broad, mostly solid Ore."

In the British Museum there is a plan of Loch Sunart dedicated by its maker, Alexander Bruce, to General Wade. Attached to this plan is the following *Narrative of the Mines of Strontian*:

" The Barony of Ardnamorchan & Sunart, the priviledg'd bounds of ye York Buildings Company for raising mines & minerals, is ye property of Sir Alex. Murray of Stanhope, who An first discover'd ye lead mines of Strontian. They lye W.N.W. & E.S.E., att three miles gradualy ascent N. from Strontian att ye head of Loch Sunart, & are rank't among ye richest of their kind in Europe. Ano he set them in lease to the late Duke of Norfolk & Company for ye term of (?) years, reserving to himself in whole for his own share one sixth part of all ye oar that should be rais'd free of all charges above ground, the said Company sometime afterward made over their lease of ye said mines to ye York Buildings Company for a valuable consideration, who accordingly are ye present possessors of ye same.

" As ye first Company found ye best and greatest quantity of Ore nearest ye surface, they therefore wrought ye Mines in open last, whence they are call'd Grooves, they also erect'd several necessary Buildings att Strontian, such as Smelting Miln with four common hearths, a Bridge upon Oaken Piles cross ye River, a handsome house for their Manager, clerks, & office, besides others for their Workmen, stores, &c. As they were ye first Planters, so they met with ye greatest difficulties. The York Buildings Company carried on their works in a more regular manner, by sinking of shafts and sumps & driving of drifts, whereby, they found the Benefitt, & the deeper they go they come into better Ore: in some places ye Vein is 3½ yards wide all spangled ore, interspers'd with a kindly sparr, & in other places it is 38 inches of solid Ore bedded in a stiff loam, the deepest and richest that has been rais'd; & by ye report & ye symptoms of ye ground, ye deeper they go, its to be hoped, ye Vein will prove richer in ore.

"The York Buildings Company have besides en-larg'd ye whole work by augmenting ye No. of their clerks, Overseers, Smelters, Artificers, Miners and labourers & their several buildings proportionally, namely four Air Furnaces, an Almond Furnace & an Essay Furnace: a smelting Miln with two common hearths, a slag hearth, a spacious storehouse, Key & cooperidge; a finish'd house for their Govr or any of ye Court of Assistants, another for their Manager, a well furnish'd Dispensary, several lodging houses for workmen in Strontian, besides another sett of buildings for them att New York, which lyes more contiguous to ye grooves; a Brewhouse, Maltbarn & Kiln, stables, workhouses, Peatbarns, & Timber & Coal-yards; & several biggings upon ye grooves for smiths, carpenters, &c., from whence they have made ye roads for leading ye ore to ye smelting milns & furnaces at a great labour & expence; besides levell'd & pav'd or laid with gravel all ye passages & streets in Strontian, whereby it is become wholesome & pleasant: they have also perform'd their part to ye Highways: from all which arise ye following Advantages to ye Kingdom all taken out of ye Bowels of ye Earth.[1]

---

[1] The late Dr Macnaughton states, in his "Medical Heroes of the '45" (*Caledonian Medical Journal*, July 1932), that, after Dr Archibald Cameron completed his studies in Paris, he "settled down among his own clansmen, and we have pleasing glimpses of him before the rebellion as attending to the medical wants of General Wade's military roadmakers, and also to the mining adventurers of Strontian."

" 1. From their constantly employing about 5000 hands, besides horses for leading their ore; & I am credibly inform'd that ye whole work is still to be rais'd to a much greater height without loss of time.

" 2. From their having expend'd several thousand pounds in Building.

" 3. From their great consumption of our own Product, such as Iron for their Milns & furnaces, & Tools: coals for their milns & furnaces; & Timber for their grooves.

" 4. From their encreasing ye Publick Revenue by ye duty on lead ore, either export'd or manufactur'd att home; & their employing of Shipping for their export & import.

" 5. From their inclosing, bringing in & cultivating both garden & other grounds, which will soon be found a greater Improvement than att present imagin'd.

" 6. From their having instigat'd & as it were infus'd from their success a desire into all Ranks & Degrees of people throughout ye Kingdom upon such and other projects, some whereof have succeed'd and severall have very good appearances.

" Whence I refer that Loch Sunart is become famous by the Greatest National Improvement this Age has Produc'd.

COROLLARY

" Therefore ye Mines conduce superlatively to ye end ye Govt has in that Great Undertaking of the Roads and Bridges carried on all over ye North under his Excellence General Wade's directions, which end is the civilizing and enriching the country. Some of these were thought unpracticable till lately accomplished. Such actions have been record'd by the faithfullest

Historians in all Ages amongst ye Masterpieces of ye greatest Potentates & Generals: which together with his Excellences prudent & steady conduct, great moderation, Acts of Clemence & Charity to several families & people in Scotland have already contribut'd more, under His Most Gracious Majesties happy Administration, to the Peace, Profit & pleasure of these parts than any subject before him.

"And however different we are in our sentiments with respect to other matters yet all Scotsmen I have convers'd with on that subject agree in the same: so that from such a good beginning and surprising Progress its presum'd a speedy & happy Period may be put to so Great a Work by the same hand, and thereupon be left in Record to latest Posterity after a suitable manner in its proper place.

"REGNANTE GEORGIO SECUNDO.
"PERFICIT GEORGIUS WADE."

Two other interesting notes in the newspapers of the same year concern Wade. The first is dated Edinburgh, 10th September:

"Letters from Inverness dated the 29th past say, That as his Excellency Lieut.-General Wade was passing on board his Majesty's Galley on Loch Ness, from Killiwhimen to Inverness, a most violent and terrible Hurricane arose, which continuing above 13 Hours the Vessel was during the whole Time in the Most imminent Danger of being drove on the Rocks and dashed to Pieces, but by good Providence and the General's Conduct, and Resolution, his Excellency with his Retinue got safe on Shore; for the good of this poor Country, whose Interest he seems to have more at Stomach, than very many from whom it might more properly be expected."

The second reference is dated Inverness, 15th November:

" Our Prisons are now crowded with Thieves, brought in by the Independent Company commanded by the Rt. Hon. Lord Lovat; who lately made an Expedition into the far Highlands at the Head of above 60 of his Company, by whose Vigilance in discovering the common Haunts of these Rogues 26 of them were secured in six Days space, by detaching his Men in small Parties, and Marching them into different Counties. But they had not that good Success in finding any Arms (tho' all Care possible was taken for that Purpose) the late Acts for disarming having had the desir'd Effect. Thus we owe our Safety to these salutary Laws and the good Dispositions made by General Wade for their Execution."

Wade left for London on 7th October.

1729

During this year Wade was still busy on his Inverness–Dunkeld road.

We hear of him attending a service with His Grace the Duke of Argyll, in the New Church, Edinburgh, where they " heard an excellent Sermon preach'd by the Rev. Mr Kinloch." Wade was obviously personally supervising the work on the great north road, for on 27th August he writes to the Lord Advocate [1]:

" *From my Hutt at* DALNACARDOCK.

" DR SIR,—Yesterday I had an express from the Post Master of Edinburgh, with an enclos'd from the Duke of Newcastle, of a very old date, which

[1] This and the following letters are to be found in the *Culloden Papers*, pp. 109-111.

by neglect was detain'd at the Post Office at least a fortnight; the letter being dated the 7th of August from Kensington.

" His Grace informs me by her Majesty's Command, that they have advice, that some of the Scotch who were with the Pretender are comeing home, in order to carry on some designs in his favour; ordering me to endeavour to discover and secure any such persons whom I may apprehend to be concerned therein, and to prevent any attempts or practices against his Majesty or his Government. He tells me likewise, that he has written to your Lordship on that Subject; and I suppose your letter may have been detain'd as mine has been. I have wrote to Willie Grant, to be vigilent towards Gordon Castle, and to observe Glenbucket's motions, who I think a dangerous Fellow, and who I believe will be ready to play the fool if he is any way encouraged by the Agents from Abroad. I think the Troops are so disposed, that nothing can give us any sort of trouble, unless with the assistance of a foreign force; which makes me very easy and free of all apprehensions from the jacobite quarter. I shall leave this place this day se'nnight, stay a day or two at Fort William, and as long at Killyhunnen; and propose to be at Inverness about ye 10th or 12th of the next month; when I hope to have the pleasure of kissing your hand; being with the greatest sincerity your very faithfull humble Servt,

" GEORGE WADE."

Duncan Forbes' reply is very interesting:

" DEAR SIR,—When I was at Inveraray, I received from the Duke of Newcastle a letter of the same Import, with what you tell me, in yours of the 27th of August, you had from his Grace. I immediately returned an Answer, That from the observations I had made, since my arrival in Scotland, upon the Countenance and Conduct of the Disaffected, it appeared to me they did not at that time know of any project to give Disturbance, or of any Emissaries from Rome being come among them. But I promised, in my way through the Highlands, to be as attentive as possible to the motions of those people, and to report with greater Certainty on my arrival in this country.

" In my progress from Argyleshire through Lorn, Mull, Lochaber, &c., I have been as inquisitive as prudence could permit; and I have the answers of some Letters which I wrote from Inveraray to Edin. upon this Subject; and the result of all confirms my former Opinion, That no Emissaries are hitherto come into Scotland; at least, that the Highlanders have not any knowledge or Expectation of their coming; and this I am resolved by the next post to signify to his Grace.

" It was because I took it for granted, that You had the same Directions as I had, that I did not attempt to send you Notice of what was wrote to me, notwithstanding the difficulty of coming at You, from the part of the World, in which I then was. But, as I believed you had the same advice, and would readily frame the same Opinion of it, I thought it unnecessary to say anything on the Subject till Meeting.

" I was so damnably tired of the Highlands, that I durst not venture on your mines. The History of me you will meet with in your Travels; I long to hear Yours. Never was penitent banished into a more barren Desart, to suffer for his sins, than what you have suffered in since your Confinement to Drumochter.

I hope, however, you have got safe out of it, and that this will find you in full Vigour of Mind and Body. I beg you may be so good as to direct John Baillie, who will deliver you this, to let me know when I may expect to see you at Inverness, since you do not intend to be long at Killiewhinnan.

"I am, Dear Sir, your most faithful, &c.,

" D. F.

" BUNCHEW, *3rd Sept.* 1729."

Considerable progress must have been made with the work that summer, for Wade writes to the Lord Advocate from Edinburgh, on 2nd October, as follows:

" DEAR SIR,—I had the pleasure to receive yours of the 26th Sept., at Col. James Campbell's, who was so kind to give me good Quarters for two days on my way hither. On the day after you left us at Ruthven, the Knight and I travelled in my Coach with great ease and pleasure to the feast of Oxen, which the Highway-men had prepared for us opposite to Loch Garry; where we found 4 roasting at the same time, in great order and solemnity. We dined in a Tent pitched for that purpose; the Beef was excellent; and we had plenty of Bumpers, not forgetting your Lord and Colloden; and after three hours stay, took leave of our Benefactors the Highwaymen, and arrived at the Hutt before it was Dark.

" The 5 dayes I continued there set me upon my leggs again, and enabled me to take a second survey of the projected Road between Dalnacardock and Creif, which is to be the work of the next Summer. I am very thankfull to you for your kind mediation of the treaty between her Grace and me. I supp'd last night with Ilay at Lady Milton's, who, I found, had been informed of the whole affair, and of our Court of Judicature held at Ruthven, and disaproved of none of our proceedings, except the last; in which, he said, he thought I had acted with too much lenity, or to that purpose. The Knight of the Bath is much your humble Servant; but more Colloden's, for he never fayles to remember him in a Bumper; though, in the main, I have interposed between him and the Bottle, and kept him sober ever since we parted. I wish you had as much influence over Colloden.

"The last post brought us no news. I shall go from hence on Monday Morning, and propose to be in London the day after the birth-day. I have not yet the honour of her Grace's Letter. If you happen to see Willy Grant, desire him to lodge the Armes that were taken from her Grace's tennants in the Castle of Inverness.

"I am, Dr Sir, your very faithfull and most obedt humble Servt,

"GEORGE WADE."

An extraordinary mistake is made by General Stewart of Garth in his *History*. He imagines that Wade uses the word "highwaymen" as a reference to Highland caterans, and not, as is perfectly obvious, to his soldier road-makers.

Wade left for London on 6th October.

In April of this year the Treasury advanced Wade £2915 "upon Accot of the Charge of carrying on and finishing the New Road for Wheel Carriages extending from Dunkeld Northward to Inverness." £670 of that money was expended on building "11 Stone bridges of one Arch."

Wade's whole expenditure this year amounted to

£3528, and his claim for the additional £613 was paid without question. That £3528 was spent in detail as follows [1]:

WAGES OF NON-COMMISSIONED OFFICERS & SOLDIERS

	£	s	d
18 Serjeants at 1s. p. Diem each added to their pay, ...	0	18	0
24 Corporals & Drummers at 8d. p. Diem, ...	0	16	0
30 Artificers at 1s. p. Diem, . .	1	10	0
288 Soldiers at 6d. p. Diem, . .	7	4	0

360 Men. Per Diem 10 8 0

Paid to the Numbers abovementd—170
    Days work at £10, 8s. p. diem, . £1768 0 0

ADDED TO THE WORK IN JULY, AUGUST AND PART OF SEPTEMBER

	£	s	d
6 Serjeants at One Shilling p. Diem,	0	6	0
6 Corporals at 8d. p. Diem, . .	0	4	0
140 Soldiers at 6d. p. Diem, . .	3	10	0

152 Men Per Diem 4 0 0

Paid to the Numbers Abovementd for 60
    Days at £4 p. diem, . . . £240 0 0
To 6 Comission Officers who comanded
    the working partyes, . . . 135 0 0
For 6 Carts and 12 Cart horses with
    Harness, &c., ... 180 0 0
For Iron, Steel, Coals, Timber, &c.,
    & for repairing the Tools, . . 90 0 0

[1] *King's Warrant Book XXIX.*, pp. 448-449.

For Carriage of Biscuit and other provisions to the Working partyes, . £170 0 0
For building 11 Stone bridges of one
Arch from 15 to 26 foot each, . 670 0 0
And for Deduction of Poundage taken
from the said Sum of £2915 paid to
the said Lieut-General upon Acct
as aforesaid, ... 145 0 0

£3528 0 0

1730

The work of this year was the making of the Crieff–
Dalnacardoch road. There was one interesting little
incident took place in Edinburgh. Wade on his arrival
in that city in the middle of July pardoned John Smith,
a sentinel of Montague's regiment, who had been
sentenced to death for desertion. Wade was living then
in Edinburgh, in the Earl of Moray's town house, and
it was at the request of the Countess of Moray that he
pardoned the soldier. The incident had a curious
sequel in 1732. The newsprints of March of that year
tell us:

" *Edinburgh, March* 20, *Monday*. Thursday next one
John Smith of South Britain, a Centinel of Montague's,
is to be shot in the Links of Leith, for Disertion. He is
an old Offender in that way, and is the very person who
a few Months ago was pardoned of the like Offence
by General Wade, at the Request of the Rt. Hon. the
Countess of Moray. He is to be interr'd in the same
Coffin then prepared for him.

" *Edinburgh, March* 27. On Thursday, John Smith,
Centinel of Montague's Regiment, was shot for Desertion. In his last words he acknowledged his having
been twice pardoned by General Wade for the like

Offence; once at Killwhimen, and lately at Canongate, at the Rt. Hon. the Countess of Moray's Request."

In this year Wade's expenditure on the Crieff–Dalnacardoch road amounted to £3520, 8s. This includes the cost of ten miles of the Dunkeld–Inverness road, which had not been completed the previous year.

1731

This year was occupied by Wade in making his road from Dalwhinnie to Fort Augustus. Possibly also about this time Wade constructed a junction road from the barracks of Ruthven to Catcleugh on his Dalwhinnie–Fort Augustus road. Wade was again advanced £3000 for this work. Here is how he accounts for his expenditure this year [1]:

"To the Right Honorable Sir Robert Walpole and others the Lords Commissioners of His Majesty's Treasury.

"The Memoriall of Leut-Genll George Wade Sheweth

"That by His Majesty's Warrant bearing date the 10th day of Aprill, 1731, the said Leut-Genll did receive from the Paymaster-Genll of His Majesty's Forces the Sum of three Thousand pounds (subject to the usual deduction of poundage) In advance and upon Account of the Charge of carrying on a New Road for Wheel Carriage from the New Fortress of Fort Augustus to joyn the great Road made in preceeding Years from Crieff to Inverness, and for Building Stone Bridges where they should be found necessary.

"That the said Leut-Genll having provided the Stores and Materialls for carrying on the Work, did employ Seven Commission Officers and 348 Non-

[1] Treasury Papers, cclxxvii., No. 24, or fol. 75.

Commission Officers and Soldiers, who began in the Month of Aprill and continued the work to the last day of October, during which time they perform'd 162 Day's Work; To this Number in the beginning of July were added 162 Non-Commission Officers and Soldiers who from that time to the end of October performed 103 Dayes Work; The whole Number Amounting to 510 Men besides Officers were paid at the Rates as usuall Viz: The Serjeants at One Shilling, the Corporalls and Drummers at Eightpence, and the Soldiers at Sixpence pr diem, over and above their pay as Soldiers, And to those who were employed as Artificers, being Carpenters, Smiths, Miners, and Paviors, One Shilling pr Diem was allowed them for working at their respective trades.

" He begs leave farther to Represent That the Said New Road is about 28 Measured Miles in length and made through a part of the Country that was Scarcely passable for Man or Horse, being carried over the Coriarick Mountain (one of the highest in the Highlands) to Fort Augustus, and is now made as easy and practicable for Wheel Carriage as any Road in the Country.

" He begs leave likewise To Represent to Your Lordships That he has caused to be Erected on the Said Road Five Stone Bridges, one of which is built over the River Spey, consisting of two large Arches and is 180 Foot in length. The other four are of One Arch each and of smaller Dementions.

" The Said Roads and Bridges with all the Incident Charges attending so Extensive a Work Amounts in the Whole to the Sum of £281, 4s. 8d. more than the Net Produce of His Majesty's Warrant as may appear by the particulars hereunto Annexed.

" He therefore humbly desires Your Lordships

will be pleased to move His Majesty that he will be Graciously pleased to Grant a Warrant for the Payment of the Said Sum of £281, 4s. 8d. as also to prevent his being put in super for the Money's advanced by the Warrant Above mentioned.

"All which is most Humbly Submitted to Your Lordships Concideration."

ACCOUNT OF WAGES AND OTHER INCIDENT CHARGES IN CARRYING ON THE WORK

	£	s	d
15 Serjeants at One Shilling pr Diem,	£0	15	0
20 Corporalls and Drummers at 8d. pr Diem,	0	13	4
25 Artificers at One Shilling each pr Diem,	1	5	0
288 Soldiers at 6d. pr Diem,	7	4	0
348	9	17	4

Paid to the above Numbers 162 Days at £9, 17s. 0d. pr Diem, . . £1598 8 0

ADDED TO THE WORK IN THE BEGINNING OF JULY

	£	s	d
3 Serjeants at One Shilling pr Diem,	£0	3	0
10 Corporalls and Drummers at 8d. pr Diem,	0	6	8
5 Artificers at One Shilling pr Diem,	0	5	0
144 Soldiers at 6d. pr Diem,	3	12	0
162	4	6	8

Paid to the above Numbers 103 Days at £4, 6s. 8d. pr Diem is . . £446 6 8

INCIDENT CHARGES

Paid to the Commission Officers for their attendance on Work, . . .	£170	0	0
Paid for ten Cart horses with harness & for repairing carts & Forges, .	120	0	0
For Artificers Tools, Timber and Sea Coal for the Travelling Forges, .	80	0	0
For the Cariage of 6 months Provisions & Stores for 510 Workmen, . .	130	0	0
For Forrage, charge of building hutts, Firing and Medicenes for Men, .	120	0	0
For Building Five Stone Bridges one of two Arches and 4 of one Arch, .	466	0	0
For Deduction of Poundage of £300 Advanced on Account, . .	150	0	0
	£3281	4	8
Advanced by His Majesty's Warrant of 3rd of Aprill 1731, . . .	£3000	0	0
Ballance Due,	£281	4	8

1732

The accounts for this year are very interesting. Wade is advanced another £3000 " upon Accot of the charge of enlarging and Completing the great Road for Wheel Carriages between Inverness and Fort William of abt 60 measured Miles in length." It would appear that Wade made very considerable changes on his earlier road through the Great Glen, for he writes[1]:

" That there has been compleated this Summer

[1] *Vide* Chapter IX.

above Forty Miles of the said Road; the greatest part of it being entirely new, and carryed on, on the South side of the Lake Ness (being a shorter and more convenient Way for a Communication between His Majesty's Garrisons) but there being above 2000 Yards of the said Road cut through a solid Rock the whole Sixty Miles could not be compleated this Year though the most difficult part of it is finish'd and made a beautiful and lasting Road for the March of Artillery or other Wheel Carriage." [1]

Wade is now contemplating the building of his great bridge over the Tay at Aberfeldy, for in the same report he states:

" He takes the Liberty to represent to Your Lordships; That he has caused to be erected on the said Road two Stone Bridges, The one an Arch of 42 Feet and the other of 30, besides two Bridges of Timber supported by Walls of Stone at each end, which four Bridges were compleated before the end of October. And as there appeared to be an absolute necessity for a Bridge over the River Tay on the Road that leads from Sterling to Inverness, being the largest River in the Highlands and often impassable in rainy Seasons, he has projected a Stone Bridge to be built upon Piles over the said River of above 400 Foot in Length, consisting of five Arches, the middle Arch being 60 Foot Diameter; and he has advanced to the Inspector £600 in order to provide Materials for carrying on the Work the next Spring.

" He further begs leave to Represent to Your Lordships that the Expence of the Roads and Bridges that have been finish'd this Year including the said Sum of £600 which he has advanced for providing Materials for erecting the Bridge of five Arches over the River

---

[1] Treasury Papers, cclxxx., No. 31, or ff. 221, 221*b*.

Tay amounts in the whole £528, 13, 2 more than the net produce of His Majesty's Warrant. . . ."

From an account kept by Major Duroure of the expenditure on the roads for the year 1732, copied into his letter-book, it is stated that this money was given to Edward Caulfield, who became Surveyor in charge of the completed roads. The same account shows that in this year £150 was spent on a bridge at "Ferragag," near Lake Ness; and £55 on a bridge at "Aberhallader."

1733

This is the last year during which Wade is advanced £3000. His actual expenses on the roads this year amounted to £4731, 5s. 9d., but £3596, 3s. 7d. of that amount was spent on the bridge at Aberfeldy. (Full information concerning the building of the bridge will be given in the detail of the Crieff–Dalnacardoch road.[1]) Wade's letter published in the first chapter of this book shows how the General left the bridge unfinished at the end of 1733. He set out for London on 21st October. The other moneys that year had been expended on the Inverness–Fort William road.

1734

Wade does not appear to have visited Scotland this year. Edward Caulfield was in charge as far as road-work was concerned, and was allowed £400 a year; and from this point there is no suggestion that any new roads were made. Caulfield's job was to repair and keep the roads and bridges in good order. This year Caulfield repaired the road from Crieff to Inverness "100 miles in length, and new gravell'd the same where it was wanting." He also repaired the Corrieyairack

[1] *Vide* Chapter XI.

traverses, the road on the south side of Loch Ness, and he harled several bridges.

1735

Wade examined the completed Tay Bridge this year, and Caulfield expended his £400 on repairing the road from Dunkeld to Fort Augustus. Wade succeeded in getting another £500 from the Treasury to pay the outstanding debts on the Tay Bridge. He further received £360, 15s. for the building of a stable for dragoons at Ruthven.

1736

Wade does not appear to have been in Scotland till October of this year. The special work of that summer, however, had been on High Bridge over the Spean, for a message from Fort William on 16th June reads as follows:

" Last Friday being the Anniversary of his Majesty's Accession to the Throne, our Lieutenant Governor, attended by the Officers of this Garrison, and several other Gentlemen, went to the River Speyn six Miles from hence, where all the Materials are being prepared for a Bridge over that rapid and dangerous River, the first Stone was laid, and the Healths of their Majesties, the Prince and Princess of Wales, the Duke and Royal Family, with many other loyal Toasts were Drunk, at the Instant our great Guns were firing on the happy Occasion of the Day. This Bridge is to be of three Arches; the Middle Arch fifty foot Diameter, the other two Arches forty Foot each; the Hills through which the River runs being very high, the Causeway, for the better Access to the Road, on each Side, will be fourscore Feet from the common Surface of the Water, which is near Thirty Foot deep. The finishing this Work will complete a safe and easy Communication from this Garrison to those of Fort Augustus and Fort George, and likewise to all the Military Roads, which by his Majesty's Command have been carried on through the Highlands under the Care of General Wade. The Company returned and supped with the Governor, where the above Healths were repeated, and the Night ended with Bonfires, Iluminations, and all other Demonstrations of Joy."

Wade stated to the House of Lords in his examination during the inquiry into the murder of Captain Porteous ("Newcastle Papers," B.M.Add.MS. 330491, f. 91): " I was not then at Edinburgh." Chambers, in his *Domestic Annals of Scotland*, vol. III, pp. 595 and 596, has the following footnote:

"Amongst the papers of General Wade, in the possession of the Junior United Service Club, is a letter addressed to him by a lady who felt interested in behalf of Porteous. It is here transcribed, with all its peculiarities of spelling, etc., as an illustration of the exceptive feeling above adverted to, and also as a curious memorial of the literary gifts then belonging to ladies of the upper classes. The writer appears to have been one of the daughters of George Allardice of Allardice, by his wife, Lady Anne Ogilvy, daughter of the fourth Earl of Findlater:

" ' I dute not Dear general waid but by this time you may have heard the fattel sentence of the poor unhappy capt porteous how in six weeks time most dye if he riceve not speedy help from above, by the assistance of men of generosity and mercy such as you realy are it is the opinion of all thos of the better sort he has been hardly deelt by, being cond'mned but by a very slender proof, and tho he was much provokted by the mob and had the provest and magestrets order to fire which th'y now sheamfuly deney nor had he the leeberty to prove it tho even in his own defence, but the generous major powl will assure you of the trouth, and yet tho the capt had thos crule orders it is proven my [by] commiserer wesly mr Drumond doctor horton and several other gentel men of undouted crided he realy did not make use of them, that there eyes were fixed on him all the while and have declar'd upon oth he deed not fire, true it is he presented his firelock in hopes to frighten the mob when ane unlucky felow at the same time and just by the capt fired which lead the two witness into the fatel mistake that has condn'd him the unfortenat pannal both befor and after the dismal sentence protested befor god and the judges he was entierly inesent puting all these circom-stances to gether the miserable state he now is in most draw your generous pity on his side ther'for dr general waid continwa your uswal mercy and plead for him and as our sex are neturly compassinot and being now in the power of the quin, so generous a pleader as you may easely persuad, considring it is a thing of great concquenc to the whol army which youreslf better knou then I can inform the duke of buccleugh, marques of Lowding [Lothian] Lord morton geneal myle all the commissioners and chiff baron are to join ther intrest with yours in this affair, by your own generous soul I beg again Dear sir you will do whats in your power to save him, thos that think right go not through this poor short life just for themselves which your good actions shou you oft consider, and as many just now put a sincer trust in your generous mercy I am sure they will not be disapointed throgh aney neglect of yours let this letter be taken notes of amongst the nomber you will reseve from your frinds in Scotland in behalf of the unfortunat capt which will intierly oblidg

> " ' Dear general waid
> " ' your most affectionat and most
> " ' obident humble servant
>
> " ' CATHARINE ALLARDICE.

" ' you would be sory for the unexresable los I have had of the kindest mother, and two sisters I am now at Mrs Lind's where it would be no smal satesfaction to hear by a Line or two I am not forgot by you drect for me at Mr Linds hous in Edenburg your letter will come safe if you are so good as to writ Mr Lind his Lady and I send our best complements to you, he along with Lord aberdour and mr wyevel how has also wrot to his sister mrs pursal go hand in hand togither makeing all the intrest they can for the poor capt and meet with great success they join in wishing you the same not fearing your intrest the generals Lady how is his great friend were this day to speak to the Justes clarck but I have not since seen her, so that every on of compassion and mercy are equely bussey forgive this trouble and send ous hop.' "

Wade supported the petition for the reprieve of Porteous, and Queen Caroline granted that petition. After the murder Wade was instructed by the Queen to proceed to Scotland, for Sir Robert Walpole points out in a letter to Horace Walpole, dated 1st October 1736: " the Queen's orders are likewise sent to General Wade to repair immediately to Scotland, to countenance and assist the government in their further proceedings."

Wade arrived in Edinburgh on 8th October. On 4th November he wrote to the Duke of Newcastle enclosing a list of people incarcerated in Edinburgh

Castle for the murder of Porteous, but stated that he feared " it will be difficult to find a jury who will not acquit those who are now prisoners."

A memorial concerning the murder of Porteous was presented by Solicitor-General Erskine to Wade in December 1736. The newsprints inform us that Wade left for London on 17th December. There are many details of Wade's interest in the Porteous affair given in Mr William Roughead's *Trial of Captain Porteous*. Two interesting details of Wade's residence in Edinburgh in that year are to be found in *The Evening Courant*. On 1st November, Wade gave a dinner in his lodgings to the " Military Gentlemen " in Edinburgh " who after Dinner repaired to the Castle, and saw the most curious Fire-works plaid off; while their Excellencies repeted all suitable Healths. After which Major John Robertson entertain'd the Garrison to a Bonfire."

The following Saturday, however, he had a bit of bad luck :

" On Saturday a Fire broke out in General Wade's Lodgings in Canongate (by the Carelessness of some of the Servants) while his Excellency was Abroad a-visiting, which before it could be extinguished, consumed to Ashes all his rich Cloathes, Equipage, &c., to a very great Value.

1738

We know Wade was in Scotland in 1738, for from the Junior United Services Club *Diary* we learn that he reviewed " five Regiments of Foot, two Regiments of Dragoons, with the Garrison and Highland Companys in North Britain." Colonel Cornwallis's, Brigadier Middleton's and General Whetham's Regiments of Foot were reviewed on 11th August at Musselburgh;

Barrell's was reviewed at Stirling on 18th, and Howard's at Fort Augustus at " the latter end of August." Honywood's and Rich's Regiments of Dragoons were reviewed on 26th September at Musselburgh. These in all amounted to some 3000 foot and some 600 horse.

1739–1740

I have found no information of Wade being in Scotland during these years. He relinquished the command in Scotland in 1740, and was succeeded by Lieutenant-General Jasper Clayton.

.   .   .   .

The following is a table compiled from all the information I have been able to gather as to the roads made under Wade's instructions in Scotland. I have given the earlier dates for the Fort William–Inverness road, although it is obvious from what has gone before that very great changes were made on the road after 1732. The estimated distances are taken from *King's Warrant Books* and Treasury Papers.

Fort William–Fort Augustus	1725	30	miles
Fort Augustus–Inverness	1726	31	,,
Inverness–Dunkeld	1727-29	102½	,,
Crieff–Dalnacardoch	1730-31	43¼	,,
Dalwhinnie–Fort Augustus	1732	28	,,
Catcleugh–Ruthven	?	8	,,
		242¾	miles

There has recently been sent to Major Mackay Scobie, who is in charge of the Scottish Naval and Military Museum in Edinburgh, and whose work in organizing the Museum deserves every praise, a manuscript giving a list of military roads in Scotland.

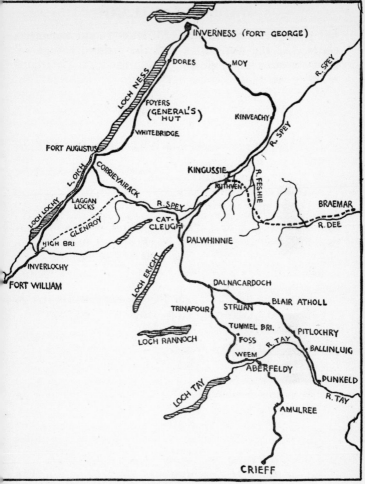

The above sketch-map shows in black lines the roads made by General Wade. The dotted line from High Bridge to Corrieyairack indicates the road or track through Glenroy, with which it is suggested Wade had something to do, while the dotted line from Ruthven to Braemar shows the line of the road he proposed constructing through Glen Feshie and Glen Geldie, but which was never made.

Mr Harry R. G. Inglis, the well-known road authority, states that the watermark and the writing are of the period 1780. The following is the list with Mr Inglis' modern spellings:

MILITARY ROADS IN NORTH BRITAIN

1779

	Miles
FIRST GREAT LINE.—Marshal Wade's Roads:	
Stirling to Inverness.	132
Roads of communication to ditto—	
Amulree to Dalnacardoch.	39
Dalwhinnie to Fort Augustus	30
SECOND GREAT LINE.—Partly Marshal Wade's:	
From Stirling over the Black Mount to Fort William, by Fort Augustus to Fort George	166
Roads of communication from ditto—	
From 9-mile Bridge to Garvamore	17
From the head of Loch Tay to Tay Bridge.	30
From Dumbarton, Inveraray, and all the West Highlands to that line	107
NOT FINISHED, but carrying on:	
From Tarbet to Crianlarich through Glenfalloch	16
Dumbarton direct to Stirling	34
Fort Augustus to Bernera Barracks and to Poolewe in Ross-shire	80
THIRD DITTO:	
Coupar-Angus by Braemar and Corgarff Castle to Fort George	111
Coupar-Angus to Dunkeld	15
Corgarff to Aberdeen	44
Castle Grant to Forres	13
Castle Grant to Aviemore	16

FOURTH DITTO, not finished, but carrying on:
Fettercairn through the Braes of Angus over
    Cairn of Mount to Fochabers, on Speyside   77
Communications from ditto to Portsoy, Banff—
    Aberdeen and all the towns on the East Coast   69
Water of Sark, near Carlisle, to Portpatrick   107

Total 1103

Wade's connection with the first great line is definite.
His connection with the second great line is that he
made that part of the Stirling–Fort George road from
Fort William to Inverness. Mr Inglis is of opinion
that Wade may also have been responsible for that
17 miles of road " from 9-mile Bridge to Garvamore "
—that is, from Wade's Low Bridge over the Gloy up
Glen Gloy to his Dalwhinnie–Fort Augustus road at
Garvamore. The only other reference to a short cut
to Garvamore is in Fraser Macintosh's *Antiquarian Notes*.
In vol. ii., page 168, it is stated that Wade made a road
up Glenroy, and on page 171 that he lived at Leckroy
while constructing this road. Burt, however, makes no
mention of this road in his *Letters*, or in his account of
the roads which he published in *The Scots Magazine*
of November 1754, and I have been able to trace no
accounts concerning this road. The only other road-
making plan that seems to have been connected with
Wade was that for a road from Ruthven through
Glenfeshie and Glengeldie to Braemar. The making
of this road was not proceeded with.

A synopsis of payments to Wade for roads and
bridges (not including payments to Caulfield for
repairs, or payments for erecting of barracks) is shown
by *The King's Warrant Book* to be as follows:

[1] For a sketch of post-Wade military road-making see Appendix.

Years of Payment	Amount			Notes
Up to 1728	£1000	0	0	Roads and other Services between Fort George and Fort William.
1729	2140	0	0	40 miles of Dunkeld–Inverness road.
1730	3528	0	0	52½ miles of Dunkeld–Inverness road; 11 stone bridges.
1731	3520	8	0	10 miles Dunkeld–Inverness road; 43¼ miles Crieff – Dalnacardoch road; 9 stone bridges.
1732	3281	4	8	28 miles Dalwhinnie–Fort Augustus; 5 bridges (including Garva).
1733	3528	13	2	40 miles (new road) Fort George – Fort William; 2 bridges (including beginning of Tay Bridge).
1734	4731	5	9	20 miles (new road) Fort George – Fort William; 3 bridges (including Tay Bridge)
1735	499	2	3	Completing Tay Bridge.
1737	1087	6	8	Building High Bridge.
Total	£23316	0	6	

Claims are made that Wade built 40 bridges. Only 30 are mentioned in the accounts. Some of the principal payments on these bridges were as follows:

	£	s	d
Tay Bridge	4095	5	10
High Bridge	1087	6	8
Garva and 4 others	466	0	0
9 stone bridges (1731)	660	0	0
11 stone bridges (1736)	670	0	0
2 stone bridges at Ferragay and Aberhallader (1732)	205	0	0
That amounts to	£7183	12	6

—which leaves in round figures £16,000 spent on 240 miles of road. This works out the cost of road-making at something like £70 a mile. The figure of £23,316, 0s. 6d. differs from the figure of £22,730, 6s. 7d. given by the late Sir Kenneth S. Mackenzie, Bart., and others by £585, 13s. 11d. Sir Kenneth does not include the additional £499, 2s. 3d. shown in 1735 for completing the Tay Bridge, nor a 1737 payment of £87, 6s. 8d. for the building of High Bridge, while he includes an extra 15s. in the 1730 payment.

CHAPTER IX

THE FORT GEORGE–FORT WILLIAM ROAD

BEFORE proceeding to a discussion of the actual line of the Wade roads, and their condition and appearance to-day, it is worth while noting one or two facts about their construction in general. (Details of particular construction and bridge-building will be given as these constructions and bridges are met *en route*.) The standard breadth of the roads was sixteen feet. But in the south the width was sometimes increased to thirty feet, while in the north we find parts as narrow as ten feet. In choosing the line of his road Wade followed the old Roman military method. He went in a straight line, and did not avoid knolls. When climbing a very steep gradient he constructed traverses. The chief obstacles encountered in the actual bed of the road were boulders. Where these were very large they were raised, with the aid of screw-jacks, purchases and handspikes, and rolled to the side of the road, where they served to mark the way in snowy weather. There was great competition between the subalterns (so Edmund Burt tells us) as to whose detachment could lift the largest stone, and on one occasion an officer was so proud of his feat that he wrote out a Latin inscription which was chiselled on the stone. An Irish rival, to whom Burt gives the " feigned " name of Hibern, hearing of this, asked another officer to compose a similar inscription to be put on a much larger stone which he had removed. The officer suggested that the English lines—

> " Hibern alone
> Rais'd up this stone.
> Ah! Hone! Ah! Hone!"

—were more suitable than Latin, since everyone could read them.

" Upon this the hero turned ridiculously grave; and, says he, ' The soldiers did the slavish part only with their hands, but in effect it was I that did it with my head; and therefore I do not like any burlesque upon my performance.' "

Subalterns evidently preferred rhetoric to oaths in those days.

The small rocks were sometimes cleared away by digging holes alongside them into which they were dropped, thus helping to make a good bottom for the road. Burt gives some interesting details of how the roads were made through boggy ground. He writes:

" When one of these Bogs has crossed the Way on a stony Moor, there the loose Ground has been dug out down to the Gravel, or Rock, and the Hollow filled up in the Manner following, viz.:—

" First with a Layer of large Stones, then a smaller Size, to fill up the Gaps and raise the Causeway higher; and, lastly, two, three or more Feet of Gravel, to fill up the Interstices of the smaller Stones, and form a smooth and binding Surface. This part of the Road has a Bank on each Side, to separate it from a Ditch, which is made withoutside to receive the Water from the Bog, and, if the Ground will allow it, to convey it by a Trench to a slope, and thereby in some measure drain it.

" In a rocky Way, where no loose Stones were to be found, if a Bog intervened, and Trees could be had at any portable Distance, the Road has been made solid by Timber and Fascines, crowned with Gravel, dug out of the Side of some Hill.

" This is durable; for the Faggots and Trees, lying continually in the Moisture of the Bog, will, instead of decaying, become extremely hard, as has been observed of Trees that have been plunged into those Sloughs, and lain there, in all Probability, for many Ages. This Causeway has likewise a Bank and a Ditch for the Purpose above-mentioned."

This explains why to-day so many of the Wade roads have a sunk appearance.

When passing along slopes, the road was usually dug into the side of a hill, rather than built up, and had a drain on the inside, any dangerous rocks over-hanging it being blasted away.

When the roads were first constructed, no bridges were built. Suitable places were selected for fording rivers and burns. All loose stones were then cleared away, and in places a causeway was made. Of course, this meant continual labour, since each spate brought fresh stones down into the ford. Wooden bridges were constructed as soon as circumstances permitted, and these in time were replaced by stone ones.

Five hundred soldiers from the Highland Companies and other regiments took part in the work. The privates were allowed sixpence a day above their pay, corporals eightpence, sergeants one shilling, and subaltern-officers two shillings and sixpence. Barrack huts were erected, and these in turn were developed into inns or change-houses, which finally became known as King's Houses. The position of many of these will be given in the details of the roads. These King's Houses were finally established at ten-mile intervals, while stone pillars were raised at each five miles.

THE FORT GEORGE–FORT WILLIAM ROAD

The tools used by the soldier-navvies were of a very primitive nature. They were picks, shovels, levers and screw-jacks, which were sent up to Scotland from the stores in the Tower of London. No work was done in the winter, or during bad weather. The road-making season lasted from the beginning of May till the end of October.

. . . .

Until something is done about putting the Scottish Records of the early eighteenth century into order, and making them available to research workers, much of the story of the Wade roads will remain unwritten. Every now and then documents are " found," which give more enlightenment. By the courtesy of the authorities of the Inverness Public Library I was allowed recently to examine a manuscript map which has come into their possession, and which entirely changes the idea that the original Wade road from Inverness to Fort Augustus ran by the side of Loch Ness from Dores to Foyers. The map has the following dedication :

" To the Honble Coll-Horsey Governor and the Directors of the York Building Compy, this PLAN of the MURRAY FIRTH containing the seacoast of Murray, Nearn, Inverness, Ross, Sutherland, &c., with all the Harbours, Rivers, Runs of Water within the said shires on the East side of Scotland, Describing the Bounds of the Woods allocated purchased by the Company for carrying on the Iron Manufactory—containing 36 Scotch square Miles exclusive of these Woods on the West and Southern parts of Scotland. Likewise all the Gentlemen's Seats, Houses, Arable and Moor Ground, Straths, Glens, Woods, Waters, Lochs, Mountains, and the respective Marchlines of each Chieftain, as they Bound one with another within the same. Also the Soundings or Depths of Water in the Murray Firth

(Lochness) and the several harbours contained in the Murray Firth, with proper directions for sailing in and out of the same. The whole being an Accurate and Exact Survey, begun in the Year 1725 and continued and done at times as it was required to this present Year 1730. By your most Obedient Humble Servant Joseph Avery."

The scale of the map is an inch to the mile. Avery's signature appears on many manuscript maps of the period. The manuscript map in the possession of the Royal Scottish Geographical Society showing the proposed road from Ruthven to Braemar is Avery's work.

This map now explains what Wade means when he states that he made a road between Fort Augustus and Fort George in 1726, and when in the summer of 1732 he further states that he has made another road, " the greatest part of it being entirely new, and carryed on, on the South side of the Lake Ness (being a shorter and more convenient Way for a Communication between His Majesty's Garrisons) but there being above 2000 yards of the said road cut through solid rock." In 1732, also, Wade spent £150 on a bridge at " Ferragag." It would have been quite impossible to have crossed at Inverfarigaig without a bridge. This Avery map shows definitely that Wade's 1726 road followed the line of the road south of Torbrack. It skirted the north side of Loch Ashie, and after passing Loch Ceo-ghlas ran alongside the Farigaig and crossed it about two miles up. It then crossed the present Inverfarigaig–Errogie road about a mile north of Errogie and continued by Loch Garth side to the ford over Gourag where Wade broke off to go down by Foyers with his 1732 road. The writer has not had an opportunity of tracing this road over the actual ground.

A Wade map in the possession of the Royal Scottish

Geographical Society also shows this road. No scale
is given, but below is a copy of the portion showing the
Fort Augustus–Inverness Road.

With the construction of the new road, in 1732, the
old one would go entirely out of use.[1] The 1732 road
ran pretty much on the lines of the present road from
Inverness direct to Dores, and so along the loch-side

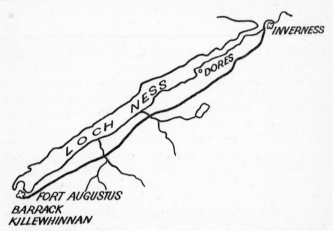

over the Farigaig and on to Foyers. One of the great
engineering feats in this road-making was the blasting
of the rocks (known as Black Rock) on the edge of Loch
Ness. Burt describes it as follows:

" There the Miners hung by Ropes from the Precipice
over the Water (like Shakespear's Gatherers of Sam-
phire from Dover Cliffs) to bore the Stone, in order to
blow away a necessary Part from the Face of it, and
the rest likewise was chiefly done by Gunpowder ; but
when any part was fit to be left as it was, being flat
and smooth, it was brought to a Roughness proper for

[1] Both roads are shown in Roy's *Survey*.

a Stay to the Feet; and, in this Part, and all the rest of the Road, where the Precipices were like to give Horror or Uneasiness to such as might pass over them in Carriages, though at a good Distance from them, they are secured to the Lake-side by Walls, either left in the Working, or built up with Stone, to a Height proportioned to the Occasion."

Near Foyers, and where the road takes a very sudden bend to the south, Wade built himself a shelter called the General's Hut. It is sometimes stated that the present Foyers Hotel is on this site. Such, however, would appear not to be the case. Dr Hill, in his *Footsteps of Dr Johnson* (published 1890), states: " Our travellers halted for dinner at the General's Hut, a small public-house nearly eighteen miles from Inverness. Here, says Johnson, Wade had lodged ' while he superintended the works upon the road.' I have seen it stated in a guide-book that on its site is built the Foyers Hotel, but this is a mistake. In the Map of the King's Roads made by General Wade, dated 1746, ' the General Hutt ' (*sic*) is marked just where the road takes a sudden bend to the south, a short distance after which it passes the church of Burlassig. Dr Garnett, who travelled through the Highlands at the end of the century, says that ' the present public-house, which is still called the General's Hut, is very near the place where Wade had a small house, which was afterwards used as an inn. It commands a delightful view up the lake.' The change of site must have been made, it would seem, between his visit and Johnson's. The old inn was on the north-east or Inverness side of the church, whereas the Foyers Hotel is a little distance beyond it to the south-west. It is a pity that the ambition of landlords has not allowed the old name to remain. It was the only thing I found wanting in this

LOOKING N.E. FROM CARN AN T SUIDHE

LOOKING S.E. FROM CARN AN T SUIDHE

LOOKING WEST FROM ABERCHALDER BRIDGE

[*page* 121

OLD WALL AT FORT AUGUSTUS

comfortable hotel. Sir Walter Scott was surprised that ' when these roads were made there was no care taken for inns. The King's House and the General's Hut are miserable places,' he adds, ' but the project and plans were purely military.' Johnson, however, was not dissatisfied with his entertainment. ' We found,' he says, ' the house was not ill-stocked with provisions. We had eggs and bacon, and mutton, with wine, rum and whisky. I had water."

It would not appear, however, that it was in the actual General's Hut that Johnson lived, because Pennant in 1769 states: " Dined at a poor inn *near* the General's Hut," which suggests that the King's House and the General's Hut were not on the same site.

Southey, in his *Journal of a Tour in Scotland in 1819*, tells of a theft from this inn. He writes: " Wednesday, September 15—left Inverness after breakfast . . . 18 miles to Boleskin, better known by the name of the General's Hut. . . . The General's Hut in which Wade is said to have lived, that is, where he had his head-quarters while his troops were making the road from Fort George to Fort Augustus, is built of mud and straw, within squares of wooden framing. If curious, or idle, or mischievous travellers had not all alike picked and scraped this into holes, the colour and gloss which have been made by peat smoke would have made the inside walls handsome as well as peculiar. In smokey kitchins the peat makes the roof and rafters black as ebony and glossy as the finest varnish, and this without any appearance of soot. The smoke is clean, and the smell, to me at least, rather agreeable than otherwise; but it attacks the eyes immediately, and that it injures them is plainly shewn by the blear eyes which are here so common among old people. A book was formerly kept at this Inn, in which all travellers, from the General's time, had inscribed their names, and many of them, as in the Albums abroad, wrote down some expression of their feelings, their opinions, or their temper. But this book was stolen by some scoundrel a few years ago. We made a good meal here upon potatoes, fresh butter and milk. Meat and whiskey might have been had, but we preferred cooler diet."

The Black Rock portion of the road was improved somewhere about 1800, for at that time £931 was spent " to avoid a steep, narrow, and very dangerous pass over the shoulder of this rock. One foot of ascent on either side to every five feet of roadway, breadth of road only from seven to eight feet. Here an empty cart was a load for a horse at all seasons, and in winter, when it was covered with ice, it was impracticable to pass it."

The Hon. Mrs Murray, in her *Description of Scotland*, published in 1799, thus describes her journey over the Black Rock:

" At about fifteen miles from Inverness, I came within sight of the Black Rock, and it seemed as if it were impossible to pass by it; In truth, it does require courage and steady horses to perform it, it being a narrow shelf blown out of the rocks; and to get upon it is by a road almost as steep as the ridge of a house, winding round a huge projecting mass, that looks as if it were ready to crush the bold adventurer who dares come under its brow; for it actually hangs over part of the carriage in passing it. Trees branching, shrubs and bushes bending over and sprouting from every chink of the rocks, towering almost to the sky; and on the right hand feathering down to the water, over a rocky precipice of perhaps eighty or a hundred feet perpendicular; and no security whatever either in climbing to the shelf, or upon it, should the horses there take fright. The scene, however, made me amends for the little palpitation occasioned by the attainment of the awful eminence on which I was mounted."

Leaving the General's Hut, Wade's road follows the line of the present road into Strath Errick. Mrs Murray remarks that " a gentleman of some eccentricity whom I met with said he believed God Almighty had made Stra' Errick on the Saturday night, and had not had time to finish it."

In the *Proceedings of the Society of Scottish Antiquaries*, 1911, Mr Thomas Wallace states that he discovered in Strath Errick the ruins of encampments used by Wade's soldiers. He gives a sketch of one of these which he found " in the birch wood opposite the Catholic Chapel. The remains consist of square, oblong, and circular forms. They show some curious combinations. Two square and one oblong one are conjoined without any apparent communication between them. Several of them are surrounded by ditches, evidently with the intention of keeping the interior dry. Each of them has a path over the ditch."

Whitebridge was the site of the next King's House on the Wade road, and with very small alterations Wade's road held the line of the present road by Loch Tarff. There are greater deviations between Glendoe and Fort Augustus. They are due to the fact that the modern road-makers have avoided gradients and bogs which had no terrors for Wade.

From Fort Augustus it is somewhat difficult to trace the beginnings of the Wade road to Fort William. It was higher up on the south side of the present road, but came down again at Aberchalder Lodge, below which a Wade bridge carries it over the Calder burn. It then runs on the south side of Loch Oich between the railway and the water, joins the present road at the west end of Loch Oich, and runs slightly below it till the beginning of Loch Lochy. It keeps on the line of the present road along Loch Lochy to Letter Finlay—now a shepherd's house, but originally an inn on Wade's road. About two miles below Letter Finlay it leaves the line of the present road, goes under the railway, and crosses the Gloy burn by a beautiful old bridge known as Low Bridge, which is a mile farther up the Gloy than the present bridge. Wade's road rejoins the present road at Glenfintaig Lodge, but some two miles farther on cuts off to the right and makes a straight line for High Bridge, which is a mile and a half farther down the Spean than the present Spean Bridge. The railway crosses the Wade road just before it reaches High Bridge, and the descent to the bridge is somewhat dangerous, though not as dangerous as the bridge itself, one of the three arches of which is now entirely broken down.

The map on this page shows the divergences of the Wade road from the present road between Letter Finlay Inn and Fort William.

High Bridge has particular fame in that it was here that the first shot was fired in the Forty-five.

PLETTERFINLAY INN

LOW BRIDGE OVER THE GLOY

SPEAN BRIDGE

HIGH BRIDGE OVER THE SPEAN

FORT WILLIAM

THE FORT GEORGE–FORT WILLIAM ROAD

Mr W. Drummond Norie gives the following account of the action in the second volume of his *The Life and Adventures of Prince Charles Edward Stuart.*

"Rumours of the Prince's arrival in the West Highlands having reached General Cope in Edinburgh, he at once took steps to strengthen the garrison at Fort William, which was situated in the very heart of the district occupied by the Jacobite clans of Cameron and MacDonald, with the two newly-levied companies of Sinclair's Royal Scots foot then quartered in Perth. The order reached Perth on August 10th, and by the 15th the two companies, under the command of Captain John Scott, son of Scotstarvet, and Captain James Thompson, had got as far as Fort Augustus, leaving on the morning of the 16th for Fort William, a long day's march of twenty-eight miles. They had proceeded nearly twenty miles along the General Wade's military road without incident, and were just emerging from the dense wood which at that period clothed both banks of the river Spean, near High Bridge, when greatly to the alarm of the soldiers the shrill notes of the pipes were heard close at hand, and it was seen that the bridge over which they must cross was guarded by a small but well-armed party of stalwart Highlanders, who, with loud shouts and warlike gestures, threatened to prevent any nearer approach by a murderous onslaught. Among the great tree-covered boulders which form the precipitous banks of the deep ravine through which the Spean foams and tumbles, other figures clad in bright tartan were visible moving cautiously from rock to rock, uttering their Gaelic war-cries, and brandishing their claymores in full view of the red-coats, who, imagining that they had fallen into an ambush, were waiting in some trepidation the orders of their officers.

"Captain Scott, as soon as he observed the High-landers, ordered his men to halt whilst he discussed the position with his brother officers and decided upon some plan to out-manœuvre the enemy. A brave man himself, he was in favour of making an attempt to force a passage across the bridge at any cost, but his colleagues, who seemed to have had no stomach for facing a determined foe, of whose strength they were unaware, persistently opposed any such idea. It was at length decided, before beating a retreat, that scouts should be sent forward to find out if possible the strength of the Highlanders, and a sergeant and one man were ordered to approach the bridge for the purpose. They had only gone a short distance when they were seized by two of the enemy, who sprang out from behind some trees, and before a rescue could be effected the two soldiers were hurried across the bridge out of sight, while at the same moment the piper skirled out another unearthly pibroch, and the Highlanders, leap-ing among the rocks and bushes like wild cats, appeared to be making ready for a desperate rush. This was more than the raw, untrained soldiers could stand, and in spite of all that Captain Scott could do the whole of the companies with their officers turned tail and fled as fast as their legs could carry them along the road they had recently traversed.

"The formidable enemy who had so successfully driven off two fully equipped companies of the Elector's troops consisted of twelve of Keppoch's men com-manded by Donald MacDonald of Tirnadris, 'a brave, undaunted, honest man, of a good countenance and of a strong and robust make,' son of Ronald Mor, and grandson of Archibald, XIV. Chief of Keppoch. Tirnadris had received orders from his chief to prevent by strategy the advance of the Royal Scots on Fort

William, and having no time to collect a large body of his clansmen, he arranged that a small party of eleven men and a piper should rendezvous at the inn at High Bridge, and there await the approach of the soldiers. Directly they were in sight he ordered the piper to play his loudest, and selecting a few picked men to guard the bridge disposed the remainder among the bushes and rocks, with instructions to rush about from place to place shouting and cheering in order to make the red-coats believe that the place was strongly defended. The clever ruse, as we have seen, proved an unqualified success, but Tirnadris was not satisfied with having merely dispersed the intruders, he was determined, if possible, either to take them prisoner, or place them hors de combat. Keppoch meanwhile had arrived on the scene with between twenty and thirty additional men, and the whole body at once started in pursuit of the flying soldiers, who by this time had been able to cover about two miles. Instead of taking the military road the MacDonalds marched rapidly but cautiously along the hillside of Glen Gloy, whilst Captain Scott followed the shore of Loch Lochy, quite ignorant of the fact that he was pursued until he had passed Letterfinlay, and was nearing the head of the loch at Laggan-ach-drum, when he found his way barred by the Highlanders, who, having outmarched his men, had come down from the hills to dispute his passage. Firing now commenced on both sides, but the soldiers, fatigued and panic-stricken, were unable to do any execution with their muskets, whilst the Highlanders, elated with success, poured a deadly fire into their ranks, killing a sergeant and four men, and wounding about a dozen, including Captain Scott, who received a bullet in his shoulder. Anxious to avoid any further bloodshed, Keppoch ran out in front of his men sword in hand and called upon the officers to surrender, threatening to cut the whole force to pieces if they did not instantly lay down their weapons. As the soldiers' ammunition was nearly spent, and further resistance in their present condition impossible, Captain Scott and the other officers had no alternative but to yield with as good a grace as they could under the unpleasant circumstances. At this juncture, Lochiel, who had received an urgent request from Keppoch for assistance, came up with a few of his clan, and finding the skirmish happily concluded, agreed to take charge of the prisoners and convoy them under escort to Achnacarry. What followed is described by James Mor MacGregor, who, in pursuance of his instructions from the Lord Advocate, reached Lochiel's house a short time before the prisoners were brought in. He says: ' That (he) the Declarant at Lady Lochiel's desire, because there was no Surgeon at the Place, dressed Capt. Scott's wound at night on Friday and on Saturday morning; and that on Sunday at (his) the Declarant's request and in compliment to him, Lochiel agreed that Capt. Scott should be sent to Fort William to be cured of his wound; and accordingly (his) the Declarant's servant, with Lochiel's servant and their horses, carried Capt. Scott to Fort William.' "

The inscription on High Bridge read : " In the ninth year of His Majesty King George II., this bridge was erected under the care of Lt. General Wade, Commander in Chief of all the forces in North Britain —1736."

From High Bridge, Wade took a straight line to Fort William. His road crosses the present road about two miles from the fort, and then comes in by the present bridge over the Nevis. Wade may have had a bridge here, but of it there is no record.

THE FORT GEORGE–FORT WILLIAM ROAD

Mrs Murray's description of passing over that portion of the road between High Bridge and Fort William in 1799 is very illuminating. She writes:

"Through the vast moor before me, there was nothing but the road to be seen, except a few scattered huts; some of them in such bogs that it seemed impossible for anything human to exist in such places. Peat-moss, rushes, coarse grass, and now and then a patch of heath, are the whole produce of this up and down waste. The eight miles from High Bridge to Fort William is the most dreary, though not the ugliest, space I had travelled in Scotland. It is very thinly inhabited; and notwithstanding its non-productive appearance, I never drunk finer milk than I did there, from cows I found milking on the road's side; and what was still more extraordinary, though I gave but a trifle more than the value of what was drunk, the honest creatures thought it too much, although they seemed the poorest of the poor in Scotland. The huts on this moor are very small and low, are soon erected, and must very soon fall down. They consist of four stakes of birch, forked at the top, driven into the ground; on these they lay four other birch poles, and then form a gavel at each end by putting up more birch sticks, and crossing them sufficiently to support the clods with which they plaster this skeleton of a hut all over, except a small hole in the side for a window, a small door to creep in and out at, and a hole in the roof, stuck round with sticks, patched up with turf, for a vent, as they call a chimney. The covering of these huts is turf, but about five or six inches thick, and put on as soon as taken from the moor; therefore it seldom loses its vegetation; as I hardly saw any difference between the huts and the moor; for what heath there was on either, was equally in bloom. In these huts they make a fire upon the ground, and the smoke issues in columns at every hole, so that if an inhabitant within be induced to take a peep at any travellers, they are seen in a cloud of smoke; notwithstanding which, the curshes (caps of Highland women) were as white as snow, and the faces of the children mostly fair and blooming. At night they rake out the fire, and put their beds of heath and blankets (which they have in abundance) on the ground, where the fire had been and thus keep themselves warm during the night. The chief furniture is an iron pot, a few bowls, and spoons of wood, and pails to put their milk in. . . .

"I had observed no beggars in the Highlands, till I came upon the moor between High Bridge and Fort William; but there, at the sound of the carriage, came bounding like fauns, through the dub and the lare (mire and bog), swarms of half-naked boys and girls, muttering Galic. Having no half-pence, I shook my head, and made every sign I could think of to make them understand I had nothing for them; but notwithstanding, one fly of a girl kept skimming over everything in her way, by the side of the carriage for at least two miles; I screaming, 'to-morrow I will give you something.' Whether she became weary, or conceived what I meant, I cannot say; but at length she took a different direction and bounded away through bog and heath, to a hut on a dismal-looking swamp at some distance. On the morrow, the rattle of the wheels again brought forth a swarm, and my skipping lass amongst them; I had not forgotten her; but all Maryburgh could not furnish me with six-penny worth of halfpence. The girl bounded before me smiling; and seemed to express, by her countenance, that to-morrow was come, and that she claimed my promise. On a steep rise she came close to the window of the chaise; she did not speak, but she looked in my face so expressively, that out came a silver six-pence from my purse, and I threw it before her. She stooped to pick it up, expecting, I suppose, a half-penny; but no sooner did her eye catch the white metal, but she jumped a full yard from the ground, uttering such a scream of joy and surprize as startled me, and might have been heard at a great distance. She then quickly turned to her companion beggars, shewing the six-pence to them, and, with a smile of delight, bounced away towards the huts with an incredible swiftness. I never gave six-pence with so much pleasure in my life; nor do I suppose one ever was received with more ecstasy."

CHAPTER X

THE DUNKELD–INVERNESS ROAD

BUILDERS of bridges over the Tay at Dunkeld have had no easy time. In 1461 Bishop Lauder laid the foundation of a bridge, which was to be constructed partly of timber and partly of stone. There is nothing to suggest that it was ever completed. Fifty years later, Bishop Brown laid the foundation of a stone bridge. The first arch was completed, and later the bridge was finished in such a way as to allow of the passage of foot-passengers. But there is no record as to when or how this bridge was destroyed. Wade intended to build a bridge at Dunkeld, but he and the Duke of Atholl could not see eye to eye in the matter. It is curious that the soldier should have given way to the landowner, but certainly the bridge was not built.

Wade, therefore, began his Dunkeld–Inverness road at the end of what was the West Ferry across the water from Inver, and you can follow it by the east bank of the Tay, until it climbs out of the Duke of Atholl's private grounds, and joins the present highroad about eighteen miles from Perth. The new part of the highroad from Dunkeld to this point was constructed much later by the Duke of Atholl with the intention of establishing the privacy of the grounds of Dunkeld House.

The Duke of Atholl had no easy time when he did build a bridge at Dunkeld. In 1803 an Act of Parliament gave him authority to construct a bridge at a cost

HIGH BRIDGE

[*page* 133]

ATHOLL HOUSE—(FROM AN OLD PRINT)

not exceeding £18,000. The bridge was built, and in November 1808 it was thrown open to the public, but everyone had to pay a halfpenny to cross it. For some fifty years everyone paid his "bawbee," and nothing was said, but suddenly an idea arose in the

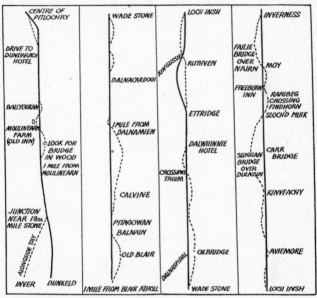

The dotted lines indicate where Wade's road does not coincide with the present highway, shown by the black lines. These sketches are not to scale, and the divergences are exaggerated. They are given to help the interested traveller to pick up the old road.

public mind that the price of the bridge must by that time have been paid for by the pontage charges. In 1867 the Duke refused to receive a deputation from the Free Church, who desired to appeal for members to pass and repass over the bridge on Sundays free. Then the trouble began.

Some sixty years ago, if you had been walking in the main streets in Perth, you might have seen a burly figure in a kilt wearing a well-cocked " Balmoral " and a heavy beard; and if you'd asked anybody who the figure was, they would have looked at you in surprise, and said: " You maun be a stranger to thae pairts. That's the great Dundonachie." Alexander Robertson (Dundonachie as he shall be known as long as there is a bridge over the Tay at Dunkeld) was born in Dunkeld in 1825. He began life as a coal, lime and wood merchant in Birnam, and his best customer was the Duke of Atholl. He made a lot of money and built a villa at Strathbraan, called Dundonachie, and here he claimed for himself the Chieftainship of the Robertson clan. But here is an old rhyme that will bring us back to the bridge:

> *The Chieftain deals in coals and lime,*
> *And the Duke was a customer for a time ;*
> *But the Chieftain's prices ranged so high*
> *That the Duke went somewhere else to buy,*
> *So, he would not pay the toll.*

Now there might be nothing in these lines, but it was Dundonachie who was chairman of a public indignation meeting about the pontages in 1867, and this meeting further appointed him Convener of a Committee to inquire into the state of the bridge accounts. This committee issued a report in 1868, and they calculated that the whole debt had been paid eighteen years before. They finished their report with a call for funds to try the case in the Courts of Justice.

Boxes were fixed up all round about Dunkeld for collection purposes. One day Sir Robert Menzies came along and saw one of these boxes. He played football with it along the road, and no one said him nay. Dundonachie answered in kind. He crossed and recrossed the bridge without payment time and again, and he, too, was not molested.

Then things began to brighten up. One morning a dozen men appeared on the Birnam side of the bridge. Two of them jumped the gates and kept the lodge-door closed, so that the keeper could not get out, while the other ten lifted the toll-gates clean out of their hinges and threw them into the Tay. They got them down at Caputh. The only result was that iron gates were put up.

A public meeting was held under the old oak-tree at Birnam, and you would have thought Dundonachie was inspiring the clans to another Killiecrankie. Armed with hammers, saws and axes, the mob, with Dundonachie at their head, marched on the gates. The policemen could do nothing, and next day special constables were sworn in. A few days later Dundonachie appeared with an axe in one hand and a copy of the Bridge Act in the other, and, after delivering a dramatic speech, he proceeded to attack the gates with his axe. After a dozen strokes had been struck, the head of the axe flew off, and a local shoemaker climbed on the top of the gates and auctioned the broken spars at 5s. 6d. a time. Next night the attack took place in earnest. Large crowds assembled and thoroughly smashed up everything.

Still the Duke was not beaten. A new gate was put up next day, but it lasted no time. Everything was smashed to pieces in the next battle, and special constables and policemen were badly knocked about.

So the Black Watch were sent for from Perth. This was the last word. Dunkeld and Birnam called out their pipers and their brass band, lined up, and marched back and forward across the bridge. The soldiers did nothing. Dundonachie addressed meetings all over the country, recited *Scots Wha Hae* on every possible occasion, and when the trouble was all over—found himself ruined both in purse and person. In the courts he slandered all sorts of people, from judges to sheriffs, and did several terms of imprisonment. But let us say one thing for him: it was due to him that the Roads and Bridges Act of 1878 was passed. The result, as far as Dunkeld Bridge was concerned, was that the Duke of Atholl was paid some £18,000 and the people got the bridge.

From the eighteenth milestone the Wade road continued on the line of the present road until about a mile from Moulinearn, where you will find a portion of it in the woods some seventy yards higher than the present road. This portion of the Wade road crosses a stream by a bridge known locally as Prince Charlie's Bridge, since tradition has it that on his march south the Prince rested at this bridge, and had a sort of march past of his troops. Another local name for this bridge is "Drochaid-nam-Bodach," but who the particular Bodach was I cannot discover. The Wade road crossed the present road just south of Moulinearn, and ran down to the present farmhouse, which in the old days was an inn. In this inn a great Scottish "road" maker died.

In 1820 Sir Alexander Mackenzie, who broke so many trails in Canada, and gave his name to a great river, was returning to his home at Avoch from Edinburgh, where he had been seeking medical advice. His coach was being driven past Moulinearn late at night when Sir Alexander was taken suddenly ill. He was carried into the inn, but nothing could be done for him and he died in the early morning. His body was taken to Avoch, where it was interred.

A Wade bridge crosses a stream beside Moulinearn, and a little farther on the old road joins the present one near Ballyoukan. For a short distance it is higher than the present road. As you approach Pitlochry you will find, where the present road bears to the right to pass under the railway bridge, the Wade road running straight on through the grounds of the Dundarach Hotel. It came out into the middle of the main street of Pitlochry, and, except where slight deviations have been necessitated by railway construction, held the line of the present road through the Pass of Killiecrankie.

Taylor, in his *Pictorial History of Scotland*, vol. ii., p. 788, in a footnote states: "In a conversation between General Wade and an old Highlander who had fought at Killiecrankie, the latter called Mackay a great fool because he did not put his baggage in front of his army. If this had been done, said the old man, Mackay would have gained the battle, as the Highlanders would first have attacked the baggage, and would thus have fallen an easy prey to their enemies."

It is difficult to be definite about the line of the original road into Blair Atholl. I am of opinion that it struck up towards Lude House, passed by the church, and crossed the Tilt by the Old Bridge of Tilt.[1] It then ran through the avenue of trees (still to be seen), down to the old Inn of Blair (now the residence of the factor of the Atholl estates). But there is a record of an early stone bridge somewhere near the present Bridge of

---

[1] In his *Chronicles of Atholl*, vol. i., the late Duke in a footnote states: "In 1734 (Old) Bridge of Tilt was widened 9 feet, and the bridge of Alltgirnaig was built." At that period the Duke of Atholl was "much troubled with demands for payment of £12,000 he had borrowed from Marshal Wade."

Tilt. It was allowed to go to pieces. Later a wooden bridge was constructed by the then Duke of Atholl to allow of the dry-foot passage of a certain illustrious personage. This wooden bridge was the immediate forerunner of the present bridge. If the military road crossed at this point, it must have continued through the present private grounds of Atholl House (the then minister's glebe, and still known as the Glebe Park) to the inn. Elizabeth Grant of Rothiemurchus leaves a note about the inn in her *Memoirs of a Highland Lady*. She writes:

" The old inn at Blair was high up on the hill over-looking the park, the wall of which was just opposite the windows. We used to watch through the trunks of the trees for the antlered herds of deer, and walk to a point from whence we could see the castle far down below beside the river—a large, plain, very ugly building now, that very likely looked grander before its battlements were levelled by order of the Government after the rebellion. Here we were accustomed to a particularly good pudding, a regular souffle which would have done no discredit to a first-rate French cook, only that he would have been amazed at the quantity of whisky poured over it. The Atholl lad who waited on us was very awkward, red-haired, freckled, in a faded, nearly-threadbare, tartan jacket. My father and mother had a bedroom, Johnnie and the maid a closet, but we three and our governess slept in the parlour, two in a bed, and the beds were in the wall shut in by panels—and very musty was the smell of them."

The late Duke of Atholl left a very interesting note about this parlour. It concerns the death of Claverhouse. Here is the note:

" Lord Dundee is reported to have been watering his

horse at a spring within gun-shot of Urrard House, and at the same time lifted his left arm to point or give some directions. At this instant he was shot out of a window through the chinks of his armour—that is, between back and breast-plate, which must have gaped open. The left side of the breast-plate inside is stained apparently with blood, and the ball must have passed out from back to front through the hole in the centre. An old woman who died near here within the memory of persons still living, used to relate how her grandfather was skulking on the hill above and saw Lord Dundee fall, and his (her grandfather's) brother, who was ostler at the Inn of Blair, saw him (Dundee) carried into the Inn, and said that the Lord Dundee died in the middle room upstairs of the Inn. I think I have seen it stated elsewhere that he was taken to the Castle, but I should be inclined to believe the country tradition."

From the Inn of Blair, the Wade road ran through the present grounds of Atholl House to Balnain where it comes down to the present road. It crossed the Bruar by a bridge on the site of the present one, and then climbed the hill again from Pitagowan. You will find a splendid portion of it if, just beyond Calvine, you climb up by the side of the Allt a Chrom Buidhe some two hundred and fifty yards. Here the burn is spanned by a beautiful example of a Wade bridge, known to local people by the name of " The Eye of the Window." The Wade road then proceeds practically on the line of the thousand-foot contour, crossing another fine old Wade bridge, till it joins the main road a mile on the south side of Dalnamein Lodge. From there it runs with the present road to Dalnacardoch. Here, as has been stated earlier, Wade had a hut. Here also was the junction with his Crieff road. The present shooting lodge, which was originally a King's House, still has on its wall the old sign, which reads:

"Hospitivm Hoc in Publicvm Commodivm, Georgivs III Rex Constrvi ivssit A.D. 1774. Rest a little while. Gabhaif fois car tamvill bhig."

Prince Charles slept here on the night of 30th August 1745, and again spent some time on 10th February 1746. Queen Victoria halted at this inn in 1861.

A fine stretch of the Wade road can be viewed from just beyond the inn by climbing a few feet up the east side from the present highway. The Wade road then continues above the present road till the two join at the point near the forty-seventh milestone where the Wade Stone stands. A notice-board, erected by the Perth County Council, informs you that "This stone was erected by General Wade when this road was first constructed in 1729." Local tradition has it that Wade, who was a very tall man, placed a guinea on the top of this stone when it was first erected. A year later he returned to find his guinea still there. The stone is eight feet in height, and four feet in width.

Two miles farther on the Wade road again seeks the higher ground, and there are two bridges of the Wade pattern carrying it over streams. But a famous Wade bridge near here has entirely disappeared. This bridge was built over the Allt Coire Mhic Sith, was named Oxbridge, and from its position you look right down over Dalnaspidal to the length of Loch Garry. I have already quoted Wade's letter to the Lord Advocate, dated 2nd October 1729, where he writes:

"I had the pleasure to receive yours of the 26th September at Col. James Campbell's, who was so kind to give me good Quarters for two days on my way hither. On the day after you left us at Ruthven, the

Knight and I travelled in my Coach with great ease and pleasure to the feast of Oxen, which the Highwaymen had prepared for us opposite Lock Garry; where we found 4 roasting at the same time, in great order and solemnity. We dined in a Tent pitched for that purpose; the Beef was excellent; and we had plenty of Bumpers, not forgetting your Lord and Colloden; and after three hours stay, took leave of our Benefactors the Highwaymen, and arrived at the Hutt (Dalnacardoch) before it was Dark."

Robert Chambers, in his *Domestic Annals of Scotland*, vol. iii., writes: " A Scottish gentleman, who visited the Highlands in 1737, discovered the roads completed, and was surprised by the improvements which he found to have arisen from them, amongst which he gratefully notes the existence of civilized places for the entertainment of travellers. It pleased him to put his observations into verse—rather dull and prosaic verse it is, one must admit—yet on that very account the more useful nowadays, by reason of the clearness of information it gives." This poet gives the following impression[1] of the Oxbridge feast. He rather varies Wade's account, since he makes out that the General, and not the soldiers, supplied the beef.

> " A fatted ox he ordered to be brought,
>   The best through all the country could be sought.
>   His horns well polished and with ribbons graced,
>   A piper likewise played before the beast.
>   Such were in days of yore for victims led,
>   And on the sacrifice a feast was made.
>   The ox for slaughter he devotes, and then
>   Gives for a gratis feast unto his men.

[1] By courtesy of the House Committee of the Junior United Services Club I have been permitted to examine this MS. poem.—J. B. S.

Quick and with joy a bonfire they prepare,
Of turf and heath, and brushwood fagots, where
The fatted ox is roasted all together;
Next of the hide they make a pot of leather,
In which the lungs and tripe cut down they boil,
With flour and tallow mixed in lieu of oil.
Then beef and pudding plentifully eat,
With store of cheering Husque to their meat.
Their spir'ts thus raised, their work becomes a play,
New vigour drives all former stops away.
The place from that received another name,
And Ox-bridge rises to all future fame."

The Wade road is quite definite at each side of the stream, but nothing remains of the bridge. From its site you get a really magnificent view of Loch Garry.

Many contemporary verse-writers expressed their admiration of General Wade's work. Fraser Macintosh tells of a Latin MS. poem in his possession written in praise of Wade. In his *Letters of Two Centuries*, p. 94, he writes:

" I have long had an address, or ode, in very faded ink, to General Wade, both in Latin and English, which I thought was the production of the Rev. Alex. Macbean of Inverness. Upon referring to it lately, I see the heading in Latin is, ' In thema, D. McBane.' The last four lines are thus:

" ' When therefore, he is dead and gone,
    Let this be writ upon his stone:
    He never liked the narrow road,
    But ran the king's highway to God.' "

Leyden republished in 1803 in his *Scottish Descriptive Poems* a poem entitled *Albania*. This poem was originally published in London in 1737, with the following advertisement:

"The above poem (*Albania*) was wrote by a Scots clergyman, some years ago, who is since dead. The fine spirit of poetry which it breathes, its classic air, but above all, the noble enthusiasm he discovers for his country, cannot fail to make it agreeable to such as have a taste for that simplicity of nature, and that beautiful diversification of epithets, which constitute the principal excellencies of antiquity."

This poem has a dedication to General Wade by the editor (unknown), and an address to this editor by Aaron Hill,[1] in which the following lines occur:

" More just thy mind, more generous in thy muse !
　Albanian born, this English theme to choose :
　No partial flattery need thy verse invade,
　That in the ear of Scotland sounds a Wade.
　When ages hence, his last line's lengthener dies
　And his lost dust reveals not where it lies ;
　Still shall his living greatness guard his name,
　And his works lift him to immortal fame.
　Then shall astonished armies, marching high,
　O'er causewayed mountains that invade the sky,
　Climb the raised arch, that sweeps its distant throw,
　Cross tumbling floods, which roar unheard below,
　Gaze, from the cliff's cut edge, through midway air,
　And, trembling, wonder at their safety there !
　Pierce fenny deeps with firm unsinking tread,
　And o'er drained deserts wholesome empire spread.
　While charmed, the soldier dwells on wonders past,
　Some chief, more knowing and more touched—at last,

---

[1] Aaron Hill (1685-1750) was an English poet and playwright, who interested himself in many commercial schemes, among which was the Abernethy adventure of the York Building Company.

Shall, pointing, to the attentive files, explain,
How, many a century since—in George's reign,
Wade's working soul, that graced his prince's
    throne,
Built these vast monuments—and spared his own."

The actual " address " contains the following lines :

" Albania's sons, may these examples teach,
How far the bounds of real freedom reach :
Teach them with equal vigour to engage
A faction's fury, as a tyrant's rage.
And see, where bursting from a Gothic night
Half her brave race emerges into light ;
By THEE ! to better being waked, they hail
Their social life, and court the peopled vale ;
By THEE ! her genius raised, with glad surprise
Sees cultured groves, and cheerful villas rise.
Pleased she beholds the golden harvests nod,
And the bold arch controul the swelling flood ;
O'er wastes the traffic-crowded causeway stretch,
And spreading hedges fence the grateful beach ;
A genial bloom of softer beauty blow,
Where kinder wishes teach the blush to glow,
While hardy youths resign the darling steel,
And melting, wonder at the warmth they feel.
With kind complacence, You, this verse peruse,
Though rough the numbers, and unknown the
    muse,
For soon, the boldest note her art can found,
Shall in a people's grateful voice be drowned."

Among other poems to General Wade is L. Webster's
*An Ode to the Right Honourable Lieutenant-General Wade,
on his disarming the Highlands, imitated from Horace.* This
poem was published in 1726. And, of course, it must

LOOKING NORTH FROM WADE'S ROAD AT DALNACARDOCH

[*page* 144

WADE'S STONE

be remembered that there was a fourth verse to the
National Anthem which read:

> *God grant that Marshal Wade*
> *May by Thy mighty aid*
> *Victory bring!*
> *May he sedition hush*
> *And like a torrent rush*
> *Rebellious Scots to crush.*
> *God save the King.*

Nor must we forget Caulfield's immortal couplet:

> *If you'd seen these roads before they were made,*
> *You'd lift up your hands, and bless General Wade.*

But we have lingered long at Oxbridge. The Wade
road descends to the level of the present road in passing
between the Boar of Badenoch and the Sow of Atholl.
It crosses the present road, and the River Truim, by
a two-arch bridge some hundred yards short of the
present bridge, rises slightly above the railway, and
then drops down on the Dalwhinnie Hotel, the southern
part of which was constructed by Wade. In this building, Cope rested on 26th August 1745, and here he
took his decision to march north to Inverness instead
of advancing to meet Prince Charlie's troops, by the
Corrieyairick road, which breaks off to the left about
a mile beyond the hotel.

The first big divergence from the Wade road is made
shortly after this near Ettridge. Wade's road keeps to
the west bank of the Truim for over half-a-mile after
the present road crosses. His bridge is beside the falls.
His road then goes to the east, by the side of Loch
Ettridge and over the hill in a straight line to Ruthven
Barrack, passing Phones House and Milehouse of Nuide.

The present road keeps to the left so as to cross the Spey below Newtonmore.

Wade built no bridge over the Spey, but contented himself with using the old ford close to the Old Road House known as Tigh na Coit. The Rev. Thomas Sinton, in his *By Loch and River*, describes the ford as follows: " The gravelly bottom, interspersed with stones of moderate size, gradually sloped to the surface towards the foot of the linn, where the hurrying, outspread stream was shallow and allowed of a ford, which was, indeed, none other than that connected with Marshal Wade's road between Inverness and Perth. For that great man did not always attempt to bridge over the larger rivers."

The Wade road crosses the present road just beyond Kingussie, and is to be found higher up on the west side. It can be traced passing in front of the house of Belleville (built by " Ossian " Macpherson, and since turned into the Gaelic " Balavil "). After again joining the present road, it is somewhat difficult to say what was the exact line of the road to Aviemore, for floods entirely washed away the original road. A portion, however, can be seen on the river side of the garage at the entrance to Aviemore. Beyond the village the road hugged the Spey. Just over a mile and a half out it crosses to the west side, and reappears again at Avinlochan, where there is a broken-down bridge. It then goes west again in front of Kinveachy Lodge and makes straight over Lethendy Hill, and can be followed through a pleasantness of trees right down to the Dulnain, which is crossed by Sluggan Bridge. Wade's original bridge was not at Carr, but two miles up the river at Sluggan. There are some doubts as to the construction of this original Wade bridge, for Sir Eneas Mackintosh, the twenty-third chief of that clan, has left it on record that "eight miles from Moy you cross the River Tunlan (Dulnain) by a stone bridge of one arch. The first bridge built here had two arches, which, being narrow and low, confined the river too much. The consequence was that a float of wood coming down the river, then greatly swelled by late rain, carried off the bridge. The builder of this one, being resolved that the same accident should never again happen, has raised the arch so high that the elevation of the parapet from the banks, which are low, is almost forty-five degrees."

The bridge at Sluggan was swept away in the Spey floods, according to Sir Dick Lauder, so it would appear that the present bridge can contain little of the original Wade construction.

Near this bridge are the ruins of Inverlaidan House, where Prince Charles spent a night. The lady of the house did not enjoy the company. In Gibb's narrative is the following note:

"Before setting out from Dalrachny, Mr Gib, finding himself run short of bread, ordered his servants to bake some, but Lady Dalrachny put a stop to them, and said she would not allow any such thing to be done in her house upon a Sunday. Mr Gib yielded the point, and would not contend with her. This lady spoke some imprudent and impertinent things to Mr Gib, viz., 'What a pack ye are! God never let me hae the like of you in my house again,' &c. Mr Gib told her it was the greatest honour she could come by, to have such company in her house, &c."

"As late as 1727," writes Sir Eneas Mackintosh, "General Wade was so sensible of the danger the workmen ran, that he wrote to Lachlan Mackintosh desiring to know in what direction he wished to have the road carried through his estate, and that he would desire his people not to molest his workmen." The estate referred to came as far down as this bridge, so we can presume that the line of the road was the choice of Mackintosh.

From the bridge Wade's road then continues straight over the hills to Slochd Muick, where it passes over the railway and keeps away to the right, until reaching the Findhorn, where Wade built a bridge (now nothing remains) at Raigbeg. Sir Eneas Mackintosh writes of the old road through Slochd Muick thus: "The descent into the hollow is so sudden, and the turn round the hill so unexpected that, if your horses are not very peaceable, you would better alight and have them led thro' it. The Military when making this road built a parapet at this dangerous turn, but by winter storms, and want of reparation, it is now nearly level with the road."

The Wade road can be traced down by Dalmagarrie to the side of Loch Moy, where it crosses to the west of the present road, and proceeds by Allt na Slanach into Strathnairn. The Nairn was crossed by a bridge about fifty yards west of the present Failie Bridge, and then a straight line was taken into Inverness by what is now known as the Old Edinburgh Road.

The actual condition of the road in Wade's time is well described by Lord Lovat in a letter to a relative[1] dated Edinburgh, 11th September 1740:

> " EDINBURGH,
> " 11*th Sept.*, 1740.

" MY DEAR (   ),

" I hope and wish that this may find you, and the good lady (   ), and all your lovly family, particularly your eldest son, in perfect health; and I

---

[1] Published in the Spalding Club *Miscellany*, vol. ii.

sincerely assure you, and the good lady (   ), and all your lovly children, of my most affectionate humble duty and kindest respects. Having received before I came from home very pressing letters from your cousin and mine, my Lord Grange, and from Mr M'Farlane my doer, to come south immediately, and sign the entail of my estate, which my Lord Grange has laboured these three years past; and he says himself now, that he believes it is one of the best entails in Scotland; as long as there is a shilling remaining of the estate, it must go to the heir male. My Lord Grange having writt to me that this was the most essentiall action of my life for the preservation of my family, I could not stand his call, so I took journey from my own house to come up here, the 30th of Jully, with both my daughters; but if I was as much an observer of freits as I used to be, I would not have taken journey. For two days before I came away, one of my coach mares, as she was steping into the park, dropd down dead as if she had been shot with a cannon ball. The next day, when I went to bid farewell to Dunballochs family, and Achnagairns, one of the hind wheels of my chariot broke in pieces. That kept me two days to get new wheels; and a greater misfortune than either of them happened to me at the same time. My chamberlain, John Fraser, that I sent to Aplecross about the purchase of the lands of Tarradale and Ridowne, coming back from that part, broke his leg on the plain road, which is a vast loss to me to this hour, for he is not yet able to go abroad, though the whole affairs of my countrey be entrusted to him. I came off on Wednesday the thirtieth of Jully from my own house, dind at your sisters, and did not halt at Inverness, but came all night to Corribrough, with Evan Baillie and Duncan Fraser, and my chariot did very well. I brought my wheel-wright with

me the length of Avimore, in case of accidents, and
there I parted with him, because he declard that my
chariot would go safe enough to London; but I was
not eight miles from the place, when on the plain road,
the axletree of the hind wheels broke in two, so that my
girles were forced to go on bare horses behind footmen,
and I was oblidged to ryde myself, though I was very
tender, and the day very cold. I came with that equipage to Ruthven late at night, and my chariot was pulld
there by force of men, where I got an English wheel-
wright, and a smith, who wrought two days mending
my chariot; and after paying very dear for their work,
and for my quarters for two nights, I was not gone four
miles from Ruthven, when it broke again, so that I was
in a miserable condition till I came to Dalnakerrdach,
where my honest landlord, Charles M'Glassian, told
me that the Duke of Athole had two as good workmen
at Blaire as were in the kingdom, and that I would
get my chariot as well mended there as at London.
Accordingly, I went there, and stayd a night, and got
my chariot pretty secure till I cam to this place. I was
storm stayd two days at Castle Drummond, by the most
tempestuous weather of wind and rain that I ever
remember to see. The Dutches of Perth and Lady Mary
Drummond were excessively kind and civil to my
daughters, and to me, and sent their chamberlaine to
conduct me to Dunblaine, who happened to be very
usefull to us that day; for I was not three miles gone
from Castle Drummond, when the axletree of my fore
wheels broke in two, in the midst of the hill, betwixt
Drummond and the Bridge of Erdoch, and we were
forcd to sit in the hill with a boisterous day till chamberlain Drummond was so kind as to go down to the
Strath and bring wrights, and carts, and smiths, to
our assistance, who dragged us to the plain, where we

were forcd to stay five or six hours till there was a new axletree made, so that it was dark night before we came to Dunblaine, which is but eight miles from Castle Drummond, and we were all much fatigud. The next day we came to Lithgow, and the day after that we arrived here, so that we were twelve days on our journey by our misfortunes, which was seven days more than ordinary; and I bless God we were all in pretty good health, and I found my son in good health and much improvn."

CHAPTER XI

THE CRIEFF–DALNACARDOCH ROAD

WADE began his great road from Crieff to Dalnacardoch from the centre of the town in the present James' Square. This highway left Crieff on the line of Hill Street and Ferntower Road, and by the north side of the present golf course, past Ferntower House. At the time of "The Forty-five" that residence was known as Fairnton. On 2nd February 1746 Prince Charlie arrived there. Fairnton was then the property of Lord John Drummond. The Prince reviewed his troops somewhere in front of the house, and later a council of war was held, when it was decided that Prince Charles with the Clan Regiments should take the Wade road to Dalnacardoch, that the Ogilvies and Farquharsons should proceed by their own country to the Spey, and that Lord George Murray with the remainder of the troops should make for Inverness by Perth, Montrose and Aberdeen. So we are now following the road that Charlie took to Culloden.

When we leave Ferntower we have a little difficulty with the exact line of the Wade road. It crossed the left shoulder of the Knock, and certain authorities state that it then went down to the back of Gilmerton, and so along the main Aberfeldy road to the third milestone. This demands an unusually abrupt left-hand turn on the road, and I am of opinion, after a very detailed examination of the ground, that the original line over the shoulder of the Knock led straight

THE CRIEFF–DALNACARDOCH ROAD

PLAN OF THE CRIEFF–DALNACARDOCH ROAD
(Scale ¼" to mile)

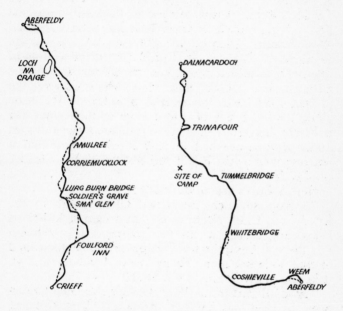

*The black line shows the present road, and the dotted line the divergence
from it made by the Wade road*

down to the gate of Monzie Castle, where remains of
the road can be seen just beyond the lodge, running
then across the Monzie road up the hill to the Aberfeldy
road. The Wade road then crosses the present road,
and keeps above it on Milquhanzie Hill right down to
Foulford Inn. Here it crosses to the west side, and a
short distance down from the main road you will find
a two-arched Wade bridge over a tributary of the
Fendoch Burn. A little farther on, the road crosses the
Fendoch Burn itself by what looks like a reconstructed
Wade bridge. Then by zigzags we are taken across the
shoulder of Gualann na Faing, and so in a straight
line over somewhat rough country till we descend by
a long incline into the Sma' Glen, where we cross the
present road near the seventh milestone. We keep
along the south side of it to a large boulder eight feet
in height, marked with the Government arrow, and with
an inscription, of which enough is left to show that it
was inscribed by the Royal Survey. " Edin . . . 1822 "
can be clearly read.

Here is Burt's tale of this stone :

" I have so lately mentioned Glenalmond, in the
Road from Crief, Northward, that I cannot forbear a
Digression, though at my first setting out, in relation
to a Piece of Antiquity which happened to be discovered
in that Vale not many Hours before I passed through
it in one of my Journeys southward.

" A small Part of the Way through this Glen having
been marked out by two Rows of Camp-Colours,
placed at a good Distance one from another, whereby
to describe the Line of the intended Breadth and
Regularity of the Road by the Eye, there happened to
lie directly in the way an exceedingly large Stone, and,
as it had been made a Rule from the Beginning, to
carry on the Roads in straight Lines, as far as the Way

would permit, not only to give them a better Air, but to shorten the Passenger's Journey, it was resolved the Stone should be removed, if possible, though otherwise the work might have been carried along on either Side of it.

" The Soldiers, by vast Labour, with their Levers and Jacks, or Hand-screws, tumbled it over and over till they got it quite out of the Way, although it was of such an enormous Size that it might be Matter of great Wonder how it could ever be removed by human Strength and Art, especially to such who had never seen an Operation of that Kind: and, upon their digging a little Way into that Part of the Ground where the Centre of the Base had stood, there was found a small Cavity, about two Feet square, which was guarded from the outward Earth at the Bottom, Top, and Sides, by square flat Stones.

" The Hollow contained some Ashes, Scraps of Bones, and half-burnt Ends of Stalks of Heath; which last we concluded to be a small Remnant of a Funeral Pile. Upon the whole, I think there is no Room to doubt but it was the Urn of some considerable Roman Officer, and the best of the Kind that could be provided in their military Circumstances; and that it was so seems plainly to appear from its Vicinity to the Roman Camp, the Engines that must have been employed to remove that vast Piece of Rock, and the Unlikeliness it should, or could, have ever been done by the Natives of the Country. But certainly the Design was to preserve those Remains from the Injuries of Rains and melting Snows, and to prevent their being profaned by the sacrilegious Hands of those they call Barbarians, for that reproachful Name, you know, they gave to the People of almost all Nations but their own.

" Give me leave to finish this Digression, which is grown already longer than I foresaw or intended.

" As I returned the same Way from the Lowlands, I found the Officer, with his Party of working Soldiers, not far from the Stone, and asked him what was become of the Urn?

" To this he answered, that he had intended to preserve it in the Condition I left it, till the Commander-in-Chief had seen it, as a Curiosity, but that it was not in his Power so to do; for soon after the Discovery was known to the Highlanders, they assembled from distant Parts, and having formed themselves into a Body, they carefully gathered up the Relics, and marched with them, in solemn Procession, to a new Place of Burial, and there discharged their Fire-arms over the Grave, as supposing the Deceased had been a Military Officer."

The local inhabitants had a tradition that the stone marked the burial-place of Ossian, and, as is usual, a debate arose among Celtic scholars as to the truth or otherwise of the tradition. Wordsworth, after he had returned from his tour in Scotland, was made aware of this tradition and decided that it should be celebrated in verse. He wrote some very moderate lines, the last of which are as follows:

> " It is not quiet, it is not ease;
> But something deeper far than these:
> The separation that is here
> Is of the grave; and of austere,
> Yet happy feelings of the dead:
> And, therefore, was it rightly said
> That, Ossian, last of all his race!
> Lies buried in this lonely place."

Near the stone, on the river side, you will see a green mound, which is said to be the burial-place of one or more of Wade's soldiers who died while working on the road. An amusing story still lingers in the neighbourhood concerning this grave. Some time in the last decade of the eighteenth century, two soldiers, belonging to a Highland regiment stationed in England, were on leave, and making their way to their homes in the north of Scotland. They had reached the Sma' Glen one evening, and sat down to rest on the mound. The traditional story continues thus:

" It was grey evening, and they had tasted of liquor somewhat too freely. 'A comrade has been buried here; let us hail to him,' shouted the more inebriated of the two, and both forthwith commenced vociferating lustily. The noise awoke Neil Gow, of violin-music celebrity, who, unperceived by the soldiers, had, wearied by his journey, on foot, from Inver to play at an Assembly at Crieff, been taking a snooze near the edge of the bank; and shaking himself, he suddenly exclaimed, 'Aye, aye, just wait till I get a sneechan!' The consternation of the reckless men of war, at what they imagined to be a voice from the dead, gave swiftness to their limbs; nor did they abate the speed of their desperate retreat till fairly within the hut of a shepherd a full mile off."

Beyond the stone, Wade's road runs with the present road till just before the Newton Bridge, where it cuts off a corner by running through what is now a quarry. An examination of the under part of Newton Bridge, which crosses the Almond, shows the width of the old Wade bridge over the stream at the same spot.

A short distance up the present road beyond Newton Bridge you will find the Wade road cross the Lurg Burn on the left by a very picturesque little bridge, and it continues up on the shoulder of Miall Reamhar till a few hundred yards short of the tenth milestone, where it crosses the present road, and crosses back again half-a-mile farther on just before the sheep-farm of Corrymuckloch. This farm was originally an inn, and a stopping-place for the drovers with their herds and flocks coming across from Loch Tay and from farther north to Crieff. It was the scene also of a scrap between a party of Scots Greys and a gang of whisky smugglers. The cavalry with the gauger had advanced from Crieff, and met the smugglers in a grim struggle near the inn. Victory went to the whisky-men. A rhyme still recited in the vicinity tells the story of the battle, and describes the treatment of the gauger thus:

> "But Donald and his men stuck fast—
> An' garr'd the beardies quit the field;
> The gauger he was thump'd weel,
> Afore his pride would let him yield.
> The Donald's men, they a' cried out,
> Ye nasty, filthy, gauger loon,
> If ye come back, ye'll ne'er win hame,
> To see yer Ouchterarder toon."

From Corrymuckloch the Wade road keeps to the left of the present road, and makes a straight line over the high ground to the schoolhouse at Amulree. The stones raised on the side of this part of Wade's highway have been used in the construction of butts for grouse-driving, and the last time I walked this part of the road it was strewn with empty cartridge cases.

At Amulree, Wade built a bridge over the Bran, on the site of the present one. Just beyond it, his road turns up to the left through the steading of Ballinlochan farmhouse. It then proceeds to climb up the shoulder of Craig Hulich, on which there is one interesting zig-zag, and the place where a Wade bridge had crossed the Fender Burn is distinctly marked. Part of the piers still remain, but I found on examination that the stone was absolutely rotten, and crumbled to dust in the hand. About a mile beyond the point where the Dunkeld road meets it, the Aberfeldy road is crossed by the Wade road, and is recrossed less than a mile farther on.

The Wade road then climbs up the shoulder of Meall Dearg, and descends to the valley of the Cochill Burn, where it has become very marshy, and is a good example of that condition of the Wade roads to-day which makes walkers describe them as " the general wade." Just before reaching Loch na Craige the Wade road joins the present road, but instead of taking the sharp turn to the left it holds straight down to Gate House, a keeper's house that was once an inn. Holding to the west bank of the Pittiely Burn, it comes in a curve into the south-east corner of the square at Aberfeldy. It then crossed the Moness Burn (earlier known as the Paldie Burn) by a bridge, the arch of which can still be seen under the present-day bridge. The old road continues for some two hundred and fifty yards along the present highroad, then swings north, and makes for the Tay Bridge.

Wade considered this bridge the crown of his road-making work. It is described in the *House of Commons Journal*, 7th February 1734, as " a freestone bridge over the Tay, of five arches, nearly 400 feet in length, the middle arch 60 feet wide, the starlings of oak, and the piers and landbreasts founded on piles shod with iron." The grey chlorite schist, of which stone the bridge is built, was brought from the neighbouring quarries of Farrockhill, the property of the laird of Bolfracks. Robertson of Struan supplied the wood, and the oak binding of the piers can still be seen when the river is low. This oak binding may not be the original, since the bridge has been repaired. Wade had two inscriptions placed on the bridge, one in English and the other in Latin. The illustrations below give some idea of the lettering and spelling used in those inscriptions.

At The Command
of His Maj.ty King George
The 2d This Bridge was Erected
in the Year 1733.
This with the Roads & other
Military works for Securing a
Safe and Easy Communication
Between the High Lands and the
Tradeing Towns in the low Country
Was by His Maj.ty Committed
to the care of Lieut General
George Wade Commander
in Chief of the Forces in Scot-
Land who Laid the first Stone
of this Bridge on the 23.d of
April And Finished The Work
in the Same Year

MIRARE
VIAM HANC MILITAREM
ULTRA ROMANÆ TERMINOS
M. PASSUŪ CCL. HÀC ILLÀC EXTENSÀ
TESQĪS & PALUDIB° INSULTANTĒ;
PER RUPES MONTESQ; PATEFACTĀ
ET INDIGNANTI TAVO,
UT CERNIS INSTRATAM
OPUS HOC ARDUŪ SUA SOLERTIA
ET DECENNALI MILITUM OPERA
AN. ÆR XÆ 1733. PERFECIT G.WADE
COPIARUM IN SCOTIA PRAEFECTUS
ECCE QUANTUM VALEANT
REGIA GEORGII 2D AUSPICIA!

The Latin inscription was composed by Dr Friend, headmaster of Westminster School, of whom Pope wrote:

> " Friend, for your epitaphs I'm grieved,
>   Where still so much is said,
> One half will never be believed,
>   The other never read."

The following quotation from *The Glasgow Herald* of 18th August 1932 tells of the renewal of the tablets:
" Major J. Stewart Robertson, O.B.E., of Edradynate,

FROM A CONTEMPORARY PRINT

[*page* 160

FROM A PRESENT-DAY PHOTOGRAPH

THE SMA' GLEN STONE

Strathtay, yesterday afternoon unveiled two new tablets, which have been placed in the pillars of the General Wade Bridge over the Tay at Aberfeldy. The new tablets are replicas of the two original marble slabs, now in disrepair, with inscriptions, the one in English and the other in Latin, which tell of the building of the bridge by General Wade, and which are in recesses in the outside of the pillars and not easily seen. The tablets unveiled yesterday have been placed in the pillars next the roadway and are easily seen and read."

As I pointed out in my first chapter, however, it would appear that Wade did not complete the bridge in the year stated, for in *The King's Warrant Book XXX.*, pages 219 and 220, a letter from Wade states:

" The sd. Lieut-Genl begs leave to represent that ye Bridge of Tay . . . proved to be a Work of greater difficulty and also much more expensive than was Calculated, which was partly occasioned by ye failure of a Free Stone Quarry and also from ye Disappointment he met with from ye Justices of Peace for Perthshire who at their Session promised to furnish Carriages for Materials at ye Country's Expense, but did not perform it. And it being built over ye largest and most rapid River in Scotland, all proper precautions were taken to render ye Work secure and lasting. The best Architect in Scotland [1] was employed and Master Mason(s) and Carpenters sent from ye northern Countys of England, who were accustomed to Works of that Nature. These with some of ye best Masons of ye Country and about 200 Artificers and Labourers from ye Army were employed for near a whole Year, the Winter season for preparing materials and ye Summer in laying ye foundation & in building ye

[1] William Adam.

Bridge. The first Stone was laid the 23rd April (1733) and the Work carried up a foot above the Pavement before the end of October, so that Wheel Carriages now pass over it.

" There remains only three foot of the parapet Wall and the Coping to complete the work which are now preparing, and will be done as soon as the Weather will permit. The Bridge is built with free Stone, and is near 400 foot in length. It consists of five Arches, the middle one being 60 foot wide. There are 1200 Piles shod with Iron to Support the Foundation of the Piers and Landbreasts, and the Starlings are made of the best Oak."

Before we leave the bridge we may take a glance back at the Black Watch Memorial, that regiment which was founded by Wade. That Wade had not a little to do with the choosing of the regiment's uniform and tartan is undoubted. In his orders to the commander of the six Highland companies, in 1725, he instructs them to take care that " the Plaid of each Company be as near as they can to the same Sort and Colour," and as early as 1735 we hear the companies referred to as the " blak Watch." To those interested in the question of the Black Watch tartan, and Wade's connection with it, I would recommend Mr H. D. MacWilliam's excellent little book on the subject.[1]

One would like to think of Wade's tired soldiers resting under the poplar-trees that line the road between Tay Bridge and Weem, but Wade's road did not run that way. Shortly after crossing the bridge, his road turns sharply to the left and cuts across the

[1] Very valuable details of the doings of a soldier of the Highland Companies who was quartered for a very considerable time in Aberfeldy are contained in *Memoirs of the Life and Gallant Exploits of the Old Highlander, Serjeant Donald Macleod.* (Reprinted by Messrs Blackie, 1933.)

low ground, joining the main road about two hundred yards beyond Weem Hotel. Part of Weem Hotel was occupied by Wade as a headquarters, as a notice above the door informs you. His road continued on the line of the present road to Coshieville. The inn there was built by Wade as a barrack, and loopholes used to be visible. I regret to write that, in the recent reconstruction of the inn, the old wooden bar that fastened the door has been removed. From Coshieville the Wade road and the present road run together towards Schiehallion, but just after passing the farm of Glengoulandie, where the track goes in to Schiehallion, the Wade road climbs to the high ground on the right and rejoins the main road at White Bridge, which was once an inn, but is now a keeper's house. The bridge here has been entirely reconstructed, on a different angle from the earlier one.

From White Bridge the present road is on the line of the Wade road to Foss, over Tummel Bridge, and up the hill by Bohespic.

From Bohespic you can visit a Wade military encampment. It lies to the left and well below the road in a sheltered hollow near a stream named the Allt na Moine Buidhe. The place is a complete ruin, but the ground-plan can still be followed. It is on broad principles the same as Ruthven Barrack. It has the same type of central alleyways off which go the small barrack-rooms. Water has been taken into the camp. There are several enclosures which look as if they had provided stables for horses. The whole district then carried a much bigger population than now, and it is worth while, when visiting the camp, to walk up the river to the ruins of a meal mill which had been working in Wade's time. The mill was known as Moulin Mhadaidh, since tradition has it that the last wolf in the Rannoch district was destroyed here. You can still trace the dam and the lade, while the remains of the stone wheel lie embedded in the earth.

The destruction of the wolf is described thus by the Rev. John Sinclair in his *Schiehallion*:

" Let me now describe, in the vivid manner of the old Rannoch narrators, a scene that was performed within the miller's little cottage. A child six months old lies fast asleep in the cradle; and the miller's wife is vigorously mashing potatoes in a black pot on the floor for dinner. The door suddenly opens, when in steps the wolf and walks up directly to the cradle. Whereupon Mrs Robertson instinctively raises the potato masher, hits the savage monster on the right ear, and kills him on the spot. The miller and the rest of the family quickly gather round the scene; the wolf's head is soon cut off by the axe and sent to Struan. The Poet Chief handsomely compliments and rewards the heroine; and the mill, with its pertinents, received that day, and for evermore, the name of Mulinvaddie."

Undoubtedly Wade and Struan Robertson must often have met in this area, for the permanent camp is no distance from the gate of Mount Alexander, Struan's home.

From Bohespic the present road follows the line of the Wade road to Trinafour. The present road there runs for some little distance alongside the river before crossing the Erochy, and then runs back on the other side. The Wade road ran straight across, and the old bridge can be seen held up by wooden supports. The road ascends by zigzags between Meall Dail-chealach and Meall Chathaidh and descends towards Dalna-cardoch. But about three-quarters of a mile from the summit a digression has been made by road-makers of a later date to the left from the Wade road to avoid

TAY BRIDGE, ABERFELDY

[page 164

TUMMEL BRIDGE

[page 165

the steep gorge of the Allt Culaibh. Wade's road holds the straight line and the piers of his bridge across the stream can still be seen. Another slight divergence from the present road occurs just before the railway, where Wade keeps to the left, and so over Garry Bridge to Dalnacardoch.

CHAPTER XII

THE DALWHINNIE–FORT AUGUSTUS ROAD

WADE's two great north roads ran as one from Dalna-cardoch to Dalwhinnie. There, about a mile beyond the station, Wade broke off to the left for Fort Augustus, and his road climbs up to over 1250 feet before descending to Cat Lodge, where it meets a junction road that Wade made from Ruthven so as to avoid taking his troops right back to Dalwhinnie when wishing to shift them from Ruthven to Fort Augustus. This junction road leaves Wade's main road just before he bridges the Truim, continues round the north-east shoulder of Crubin Beag, and so runs by Caraldie, whence it proceeds on the line of the present road to the junction at Cat Lodge, sometimes called Cat Cleugh.

From this junction the Wade road again keeps the line of the present road to Drumgask, whence it runs for less than a mile along the Laggan Road. There you will find it going into a field on the right, crossing the Mashie burn and keeping on the south side of the Spey by Shirrabeg and Shirramore to Garvamore, a keeper's house which was at one time an inn. It was about a mile up from the main road junction that was the farthest point reached by Cope's outposts before that general decided at Dalwhinnie to make for Inverness instead of advancing to meet the Jacobites on the Corrieyairack. The pretty Roman Catholic chapel that you pass on the road was built by the Macnabs

166

of Dalchully. The road then crosses the Spey by St George's Bridge, a two-arched erection completed by Wade in 1732. The length of the bridge is 150 feet, each arch is 40 feet, and the centre pier rests on a rock in the middle of the river.

The road then continues by the north side of the

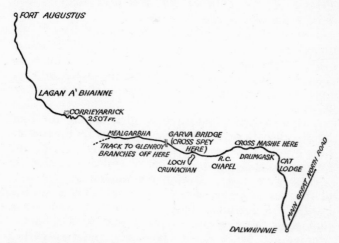

Spey to Meall Garbha, where a track breaks off to the left which takes you by Loch Spey and over the col into Glenroy and so to Fort William. In early days there was some considerable population at this point, and in 1637 there was at least one family living here, who carried on business as wool-merchants.

The Wade road keeps to the east of the Yairack stream, and then by a series of zigzags climbs through the pass of Corrieyairack. Originally the ascent was made by seventeen traverses varying in length from seventy to eighty yards, but these have been reduced to thirteen. Each traverse was buttressed on the outside by a stone wall ten to fifteen feet high, and flanked on the inside by a drain. From the top of the pass the road runs by the side of the Allt Coire Ucdachan, and crosses a tributary of the Tarff, the Allt Lagan-a-bhainne. The old bridge here was broken down many years ago and the ford is dangerous. Walkers are greatly in the debt of the volunteer workers who rebuilt this bridge two years ago.

Chambers, in his *Domestic Annals*, vol. iii., p. 562, publishes an interesting letter signed by N. Macleod, who, Chambers thinks, was the laird of Dunvegan. This Macleod was crossing the Corrieyairack in 1731, and he writes to the newspapers of the day as follows:

" Upon entering into a little glen among the hills, lately called Laggan a Vannah, but now by the soldiers Snugburgh, I heard the noise of many people, and saw six great fires, about each of which a number of soldiers were busy. During my wonder at the cause of this, an officer invited me to drink their majesties' healths. I attended him to each fire, and found that these were the six working-parties of Tatton's, Montague's, Mark Ker's, Harrison's, and Handyside's regiments, and the party from the Highland Companies, making in all about five hundred men, who had this summer, with indefatigable pains, completed the great road for wheel-carriages between Fort Augustus and Ruthven. It being the 30th of October, his majesty's birthday, General Wade had given to each detachment an ox-feast, and liquor; six oxen were roasted whole, one at the head of each party. The joy was great, both upon the occasion of the day, and the work's being completed, which is really a wonderful undertaking."

From this point the Wade road drops into the valley

of the Tarff and continues right down past Cullachy House into Fort Augustus.

The Corrieyairack went out of use altogether over a hundred years ago. The Hon. Mrs Murray leaves an exciting account of a journey across it by coach in 1798. She writes:

"As we were sitting at breakfast with the good governor at Fort Augustus, an Oxonian sent in his name, begging leave to see the fort. He had permission, and was invited to breakfast; he was a very genteel young man, and gave us some account of his tour. . . . At Dalwhinnie, the road to Fort Augustus over Corryarraick branches from the great Inverness road. None of this young gentleman's party dared to encounter that road, except himself and servant, on horseback; the rest went on to Inverness by the great road. The day he crossed Corryarraick was a continued violent rain and storm of wind, which gave it the appearance of wild desolation, beyond anything he could describe; and the whole of the road itself, he said, was rough, dangerous and dreadful, even for a horse. The steep and black mountains, and the roaring torrents, rendered every step his horse took, frightful; and when he attained the summit of the zigzag up Corryarraick, he thought the horses, himself, man and all would be carried away, he knew not whither; so strong was the blast, so hard the rain, and so very thick the mist; and as for cold, it stupified him. He thought it almost a miracle to escape unhurt from such horrid wastes, roaring torrents, unwholesome vapour, and frightful fogs; drenched from top to toe, frozen with cold, and half dead with fatigue. He said he had heard people had gone that pass in a carriage, but he was sure it was impossible. The governor's family assured him it was done frequently; and turning to me, said, 'here is one who means to do so to-morrow, in a chaise.' The gentleman stared, and added, ' Then I must alter my journal, for I thought it impossible.' A young lady present said, she had crossed the mountain on horseback in winter, when snow was on the ground, but it was hazardous. Many, by imprudence, have there lost their lives in winter; and some indeed from fatigue and cold; particularly one poor woman, attending on a marching troop, carrying an infant in her arms. At the top of the mountain she sank, and would not be persuaded to be removed, nor suffer the child to be taken from her. She fell asleep, and the people who were sent the next morning from the fort to seek for her, found her sitting against a stone, nearly covered with snow. The woman was quite dead; but the infant at her breast, being entirely covered with snow, was not absolutely lifeless. It was carried to the fort, where the governor's lady (from whom I had the sad tale) restored it to life; but it did not recover the perfect use of its limbs for many weeks, so much were they frozen. Soldiers, too, in their march, have often perished there, by imprudently drinking quantities of spirits at the inn on the Moor, thinking thereby to keep out the cold; but alas! it was the sure way to destruction.

" All these accounts did not deter me from going over the pass. I wished to see it, and I had come back from Fort William on purpose. . . . My postillion had been over the pass in May: he said, though the road was bad and rough, he could drive me over it with safety; and if I could get a pair of horses to put to those I had to help to draw us up the hill, it would be of far more use than the assistance of all the invalids in the fort. I followed his advice. The smith carefully examined the carriage, put all right that was wrong, and the morning looking tolerable, at eight o'clock I took leave of my good friends in the fort, and drove to the inn, where they added two plough horses, harnessed with ropes, to mine. The road over Corryarraick quits the Fort William road about a mile and a half from the inn; and immediately begins to wind amongst and up the district of mountains to the south-east of Fort Augustus. . . . The first seven miles of ascent are not positively on the sides of Corryarraick; but of other mountains nearly equal in height. It is not till after the crossing the bridge over the river Tarff, at the hollow, called in Galic Laga-ne-viene, the hollow of milk, that the base of Corryarrick begins. All these mountains afford fine pasture for sheep, and are at present nothing but sheep-farms; though formerly both black cattle and sheep were raised on them. There being some wood hanging about the broken banks of the Tarff, the descent to the bridge is very pretty; but crossing it, and mounting the narrow steep way on the opposite side, I preferred the safety of my own legs to a reliance on the horses. . . . From the base of Corryarraick to its summit, the road lies on a broad side of it. The ascent is to be sure very long and steep, but not excessively so; nor does the hill sweep from the road very precipitately to a stream below, which is at a considerable distance from it. The mountain on the left rises high; and on each side of the passing track is a stony rough pasture, mixed with rushes, and a black boggy-looking heath down to the stream; on the other side of which, the mountains have the same hue as that I was ascending. Not a shrub, or bush, to be seen, nor trace of a house, except two or three huts at Laga-ne-veine; so that the scene at all times, and in all weathers, must be black and dreary. Long poles are driven into the ground, by the edge of the road, at stated distances, all the way up the ascent; and also down the zigzag on the other side, in order to mark the track, in the season of snow. Just at the winding to attain the summit, there is a degree of precipice, but neither perpendicular nor very dangerous, unless for a phaeton in a high wind; as one was actually blown from thence, and turned over and over, down the mountain, the year before I saw Corryarraick. Having arrived at the top, where there is a small plain, of perhaps half a mile, I got out of the chaise, that I might be a judge of the climate there. It was certainly cold enough for my great coat; but I became neither torpid nor frozen. I discharged my plough horses. . . . When I came to the beginning of the zigzag, the sun began to shine; and to the south-west, above the rest of the mountain ocean's waves, I saw Ben Nivis, which I distinguished from the other mountains; it being rendered conspicuous by the sun shining upon its white patches of snow. At the commencement of the zigzag I got out of the carriage, and walked down at my leisure; amusing myself by picking up curious stones and pebbles in the channels made by the torrents, which cross the road at every five or ten yards. Round the base of the mountain, at some distance from the zigzag, is a stream, into which the other torrents dash; leaving behind them broad channels of smooth round stones, washed from the higher parts. The road is so cut up by these violent torrents, from the top of the zigzag to the entrance on the plain, that for four or five miles scarcely ten yards can be found free of them; which is, indeed, sufficient to pull a slight carriage to pieces. Allen led the horses, and the wheels being dragged, he came quietly and safely to the bottom of that extraordinary pass. . . .

" At the foot of the zigzag, I looked up the mountain

FROM ABOVE

FROM BELOW

LOOKING TOWARDS THE SPEY FROM THE CORRIEYAIRACK ZIGZAGS

of Corryarraick with astonishment, to think, that by a distance of only a mile and a half, I had descended an eminence that was full nine miles to climb on the other side. I longed, but I longed in vain, for the effect of a moving zigzag, such as was described by my friend Major Barry. One part of the 24th regiment, in which he served in the year 1746, was, on a fine sun-shining day, marching from Fort Augustus over Corryarraick. The officers, to add to the uncommonness of the scene, ordered the men to walk one by one down the zigzag; and the baggage and women to bring up the rear on horseback. What an extraordinary appearance in such a desert! To see a military moving zigzag of almost two miles; their arms glittering in the summer sunbeams, shining full upon them, and their officers at the bottom admiring the sight. I had not the pleasure of seeing a living being there, except the men and horses with the chaise, slowly creeping down the curious ridge: but in my mind's eye, I saw the Major's troops; I beheld their arms glitter; the women mounted, bringing up the rear; and he himself by my side, in raptures at the effect of their plan."

As I have written, the road went out of use over one hundred years ago; but Mr Ian Macpherson, of Half-way House, Dalwhinnie, whose father lived in Garva-more, informed me that the last horses to be driven to Falkirk came over Corrieyairack in 1890, that cattle were driven over it till 1896 and sheep till 1899.

Prince Charlie, when he came south across the Corrieyairack, approached it from Aberchalder, and reached the road above the great pass which is known as the Larig More, and which led down to Glen Turret and Glenroy. At the point where the Young Chevalier reached Wade's road there is a green hillock sur-rounded by a trench. History has it that here the

Jacobite officers had a meal, and the hillock is known as "Prince Charlie's Dining-Table." The area round Lagan-a-bhainne is the site of the old summer shielings of the people of Killichiumen, while Trappaud, one of the governors of Fort Augustus, used to run a market-garden there.

I have written of the Roman Catholic Chapel which lies by the side of our road just beyond Drumgask. Among famous priests who ministered there was Father Donald Forbes. Father Forbes, in the course of his duties, made many hazardous crossings of the Corrieyairack. One of the most remarkable was completed on 27th December 1819. The good father had taken with him on this occasion four men and a pony. So deep was the snow that they lost their way. They left it to the pony to find the road, the men following behind in single file, each holding on to the other, and the foremost to the pony's tail. So they came safely to their destination.

For the information of walkers, the distances across the Corrieyairack to-day are as follows:

Fort Augustus to Lagan-a-bhainne	.	7 miles
Lagan-a-bhainne to Summit	. .	2½ miles
Summit to Meall Garbha	. . .	4 miles
Meall Garbha to St George's Bridge	.	5 miles

CHAPTER XIII

PLANS FOR THE FUTURE

That Wade, or his staff, planned other roads between 1734–1740 there can be no doubt. But that nothing was done beyond the planning is also certain. The series of Wade maps possessed by the Royal Scottish Geographical Society show a suggestion for a road from Fort William by Kinlochleven and the Devil's Staircase to Glencoe and so to the south. Another plan shows the line of a proposed road from Ruthven Barrack to the Castle of Mar by Glen Feshie and Glen Geldie. In time the Devil's Staircase road was made by the military, but nothing was ever done by soldiers or civilians to the Glen Feshie road. To this day Scotland is crying for the completion of the great junction road from Aberdeen to Oban, and it may not be out of place to consider how this road could be made along Wade's suggested route. As it is, the walk from the Linn of Dee to Ruthven Barrack is a very fine one, and the following notes on the construction of this road may be of interest to the walker.

The conditions at the moment are as follows. The fifty-eight miles from Aberdeen to Braemar are covered by a perfectly good road. What might be termed a second-class road takes up the next six miles to the Linn of Dee. Then we follow a road which for seven miles bit by bit degenerates into a mere cart-track at the point where it crosses the Geldie to Geldie Lodge.

There are then nine miles of a foot-track over the watershed to Glenfeshie Lodge. A very poor road covers the next ten miles to Kingussie, where we meet the Great North Road.

What therefore would require to be done would be the standardizing of the existing rough roads between, on the east, the Linn of Dee and Geldie Lodge and, on the west, Kingussie and Glenfeshie Lodge, a total distance of seventeen miles—and nine miles of entirely new road construction between Geldie Lodge and Glenfeshie Lodge.

There is no demand for a great engineering feat to complete the new construction. In the first place, the route is the natural pass. It lies between the Atholl hills and the great Cairngorm cluster. In fact, there is a persistent idea that at the Sgarsoch—a hill just south of Geldie Lodge—a cattle market was held, the fore-runner of the Crieff and the Falkirk trysts. This is not to be wondered at, for from this point are openings by Glen Tilt to Perthshire, by Glen Feshie to Inverness-shire, and by Glen Geldie to Aberdeenshire. It would appear that here is a bit of the lost economic history of Scotland.

In the second place, the level of the summit of the pass is not a high one. The road at the Linn of Dee is 1250 feet above sea-level, Geldie Lodge is just on the 1750 line, and from that point there is a gradual rise to the summit of less than 100 feet. In the six-odd miles to Glenfeshie Lodge there is a drop of 650 feet, again fairly gradual. You cross the Dee, the Eidart and the Feshie. There is no obstacle to the construction of proper bridges over these rivers.

So let us now take a walk over the new road from the Linn to Kingussie. After crossing the bridge at the Linn we turn to the left. Keeping the line of the Dee, but on a much higher level, we first pass two larachs, one of which (Dail a' Mhoraire Mhor) is said to be the place where Dundee camped on his way to the end at Killiecrankie. We then drop down on the river, and come to White Bridge, where we cross the Dee. Near here can be seen the remains of houses which mark the Dubrach. In Braemar graveyard there is a tombstone on the grave of " Peter Grant, sometime farmer in Dubrach, who died at Auchindryne, 11th February, 1824, aged 110 years." Grant was the last of the " Forty-five rebels."

In the barn of Dubrach, a picket of Government troops was stationed after the Forty-five. This picket patrolled from Dubrach south-east into the hills, crossed Glen Christie and Glen Connie to Gleney, and proceeded south to the top of that glen. There they met a picket patrolling from Glen Shee westwards. Sergeant Arthur Davies, of Guise's regiment, was stationed during the summer of 1749 with a detachment of men at Dubrach. John Michie, in his *Deeside Tales*, gives the following details of what happened to Davies :

" Twice a week it was Davies' duty to patrol the hills to the south and south-east, and meet about the head of Gleney a similar party whose headquarters were in Glen Shee. His beat thus traversed a wild and remote country. To Davies, however, the solitude had a particular attraction as affording him the better opportunity of a shot at the deer, of which sport he was passionately fond.

" Besides being a sportsman, Davies was a considerable dandy. He was dressed in a blue coat and a vest of ' stript lutstring,' wore two gold rings on his fingers, large silver buckles on his shoes, silver knee-buckles, two dozen silver buttons on his vest, and carried a silver watch with a silver seal, and a purse

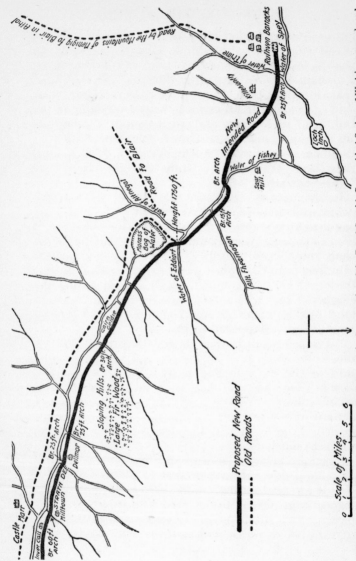

The labels visible in the map include:

Castle Marr
Inver Call
Br. 60 ft. Arch
EASTERN DEE
Miltown
Dalmor
Br. 25 ft. Arch
Br. 25 ft. Arch
Br. 30 ft. Arch
Sloping Hills
Large Fir Woods
Corarie
Road to Blair
Allt. Sheanagal
Morass Bog of Water
Waters to Vivagal
Height 1750 ft.
Water of Eddart
New Intended Road
Br. Arch
Br. 15 ft. Arch
Allt. Fheannagan
Water of Fishey
Saw Mill
Allt. Mhuinn
Ruthven Barracks
Water of Spey
Br. 25 ft. Arch
Loch Inch
Road by the Mountains of Fravigg to Blair in Athol

Proposed New Road
Old Roads

Scale of Miles.
0 ½ 1 2 3 4 5 6

This is a reproduction on a reduced scale of the map in the possession of the Royal Scottish Geographical Society of Wade's proposed road through Glen Feshie. Mr John Mathieson, the Society's map curator, made the copy from which this block is produced. He inserted with fifteen and a half gold guineas in his pocket. Such a figure must have been something of a novelty on the hills of Braemar.

" Thus accoutred, the unfortunate man left Dubrach before daybreak on the 28th September, followed soon after by four privates of the post. He had his gun and ammunition with him, his intention being to keep at some distance from the men and ' follow his sport.' All of them made for Gleney, and the rendezvous with the Glenshee party. Soon after sunrise John Grower, Inverey, came across Davies in Glen Connie. . . . Going on his way, Davies is next heard of at the head of Gleney, where he met the Glenshee corporal. After some talk, they parted, each of them setting out on the return journey to his headquarters. The four privates had completed the round by four o'clock, reaching Dubrach again at that hour, but Davies never returned, and, as far as his friends could learn, never was seen again.

" The night before the day when he disappeared, two men, Duncan Terig, alias Clerk, and Alex. Bain MacDonald, had slept in a house owned by a John Grant in Gleney. Clerk's father was farmer in Milton of Inverey not far off; MacDonald was forester to Lord Braco, and lived in Allanaquoich on the other side of the Dee. According to Grant, they rose early in the morning and set off to the hills (where Davies also was hunting) after deer. Both carried guns, though only MacDonald had permission to do so, and Clerk wore the forbidden plaid, a grey tartan with red in it. Suspicion fell on these two as the murderers of Davies, but it was not till 1754, five years after, that they were brought to trial. The Crown relied mainly on the evidence of two witnesses and on certain suspicious circumstances. Clerk's sweetheart was said to have been seen wearing Davies' rings, and some of his property was traced to MacDonald's possession. Clerk also, ' though he was not possesst of any visible funds or effects which could enable him to stock a farm before the period of the murder, yet soon thereafter took a lease of farms,' for which he paid a considerable rental. But other evidence made out his father to be a man of means.

" The first witness was a young man Macpherson alias MacGillas, in Inverey. The story he told was peculiar. About a year after the Englishman's disappearance, he said, a vision of a man appeared to him announcing himself as the ghost of Sergeant Davies, and requesting him to go to the hill of Cristie in Gleney and bury his bones. On his asking who had committed the murder he got the answer that it was Clerk and MacDonald. At the specified spot he found human remains, which he recognized from the clothing and other things to be those of the sergeant. The rings, silver ornaments and money were all gone. On being asked what language the ghost spoke in, Macpherson replied, ' In as good Gaelic as ever I heard in Lochaber.'

" The next witness, Angus Cameron, a man of Rannoch in Perthshire, had a more straightforward story to tell. In the year of the murder he had been living by the cateran trade. He belonged to a band which operated far and wide over the country. On the night of the 27th September, he and a companion had slept in Glenbruar braes, ten miles distant from the scene of the murder, had risen before daybreak, and made their way to the hill of Cristie, where they had arranged to meet their leader and others of the band from Lochaber. Whatever their business was (and though Cameron does not say, there is little difficulty in supposing that a cattle-lifting job was on hand), it required secrecy. They lay hidden for the day in a hollow on the hill, keeping a look-out for their expected companions. About mid-day, Duncan Clerk (whom Cameron was acquainted with) and another man passed so close to them that Cameron easily recognized them, but they continued to lie quiet in their hiding-place. Later in the day, about an hour and a half before sunset, they caught sight of a man in blue, with a gun in his hand, within gunshot distance of them. Cameron's account of the scene that was then enacted runs as follows: ' That he saw Clerk and his companion meet with the man in blue; and, after they had stood for some time together, he saw Clerk strike at the man in blue, as he thought, with his naked hand only, upon the breast; but, upon the stroke, he heard the man struck cry out, and clap his hand upon the place, turn about and go off; that Clerk and the other man stood still for a little and then followed after, and he saw the said Duncan and the other man, each of whom had a gun, fire at the man in blue and immediately he fell.' This thrilling spectacle, thrown in such a surprising manner before their eyes, was too serious for the caterans; they immediately got up and bolted, leaving the two men handling the dead body.

" In spite of this evidence, the Edinburgh jury were not satisfied of the prisoners' guilt. The counsel for the defence fastened, of course, on the ghost story and made great play with the English sergeant speaking ' good Lochaber Gaelic,' though, as Sir Walter Scott remarks, there was nothing more ridiculous in a ghost speaking a language which he did not understand when in the body than there was in his appearing at all. Anyhow, Clerk and MacDonald were assoilzied *simpliciter* and dismissed from the bar.

"Such were the circumstances under which Davies met his death, as far as they can be gathered from the published account. A careful reading of the evidence, however, leaves the impression that more might have been produced against the prisoners. Tradition enables us to complete the story.

"They were, as their advocate was convinced, guilty. Clerk, who was a determined and fearless man, was the prime mover; MacDonald, it is said, never fired at all. The people who were shearing their corn in Gleney had seen them setting out with their guns, and the spot where the deed was done was at no great distance from where they were working; indeed the shots are said to have been heard by them. Macpherson at any rate, who happened to be on the hill, heard the firing close beside him and thought the hunters had shot a deer. Running forward over a hillock which obstructed his view, he was horrified to find them engaged in robbing a dead body. Clerk immediately ordered him to take a share of the spoil, and threatened to shoot him if he did not. Macpherson fled precipitately, and managed to escape owing to the fortunate interference of his dog, which seized and held Clerk.

"Scott's explanation of the ghost story agrees with the account current in Braemar. According to the traditionary record, Macpherson had tried blackmailing Clerk, and, whether it was on the failure of this or from a more worthy motive, he determined to reveal what he knew. He felt that the sentiment of the country, though it did not actively approve of the murder, was in favour of letting sleeping dogs lie. He, therefore, invented the story of Davies' apparition having visited him and ordered him to bury his bones, well knowing that according to current Highland belief a ghost's commands must be obeyed whatever they might be."

But to return to the road. When we cross the Dee and leave it at White Bridge, we pass on our right Carngeldie, where a Dalmore laird buried a fortune under a stone on which he cut the figure of a horseshoe —a fortune that tradition says will be discovered only by a man called Red Roderick, whose father and mother are both MacKenzies, and who will reach the treasure some misty morning when on the track of a strayed ox.

Where the Geldie turns sharply to the right we can look south to the Bynach shieling, to the march of Mar and Atholl, to the opening of Glen Tilt, and there, clearly displayed, is Carn nan Gabhar, the highest peak of Beinn a' Ghlo.

The Glen of the Geldie is not imposing as far as scenery goes. It is a wide glen of bare moorland. Glengeldie Lodge comes into view on the other side of the stream, but our road does not cross the Geldie. Here we come to the footpath, not at all distinct. It is somewhat difficult to tell just where we cross the highest point, but about a mile below it we reach the Eidart, close to where that river joins the Feshie. The Feshie has a somewhat extraordinary course. First of all, it flows due east, and to all normal appearances is making its way to the Dee Valley, when it suddenly takes a bend to the west, and descends to the Spey Valley. Undoubtedly the original outlet of the Feshie was to the Dee, but we have here a very good example of what is known geologically as "river-capture."

The Eidart can usually be crossed near the junction to the Feshie, and the bridle-path now takes us down into Glen Feshie, which has an impressive gateway made by the two hills, Craig-na-Caillich and Creag-na-Gaibhre.

The glen as it descends towards Feshie Lodge is very

beautiful, with birches, aspens, pines and junipers. We soon come to the ruins of a number of buildings erected by the Duchess of Bedford when she was a shooting-tenant in the forest. On the fireplace of one of these huts Landseer sketched a picture of three stags and a hind. A Mackintosh of Mackintosh had this fireplace covered over by a building so that the drawings might be preserved. We leave the Feshie just over from Achlean, where lived the fox-hunter whose dogs appear in so many of Landseer's paintings. And so we come by Tromie Bridge to Ruthven Barrack.

CHAPTER XIV

BACK TO THE BATTLEFIELDS

On 2nd July 1739 George Wade was made a full
General; on the 1st of May in the following year he
was relieved of his command in Scotland, and was
succeeded by General Clayton. It would appear that
during that interval Wade was employed training
troops for the war which had broken out with Spain.

In the beginning of 1742 Wade was appointed
Lieutenant-General of the Ordnance, and later in the
same year a Privy Councillor. In 1732 he had been
made Governor of Berwick and Holy Island, and a
year later he had been appointed Governor of Fort
William, Fort Augustus and Fort George, which
positions he retained till his death. He was also Colonel
of the 3rd Dragoon Guards, and his emoluments must
have been of very considerable dimensions. In fact,
he seems always to have had plenty of money. As has
been pointed out, he was a shareholder in the Strontian
mines, and he had been in a position to lend the Duke
of Atholl £12,000. On 14th December 1743 he was
made a Field-Marshal, and as Horace Walpole writes:
" Wade is to have the command of the Army, as it is
supposed, on the King's not going abroad."

But, before this last appointment, Wade was to
renew his connection with Scotland. Despite the strong
protest made by Duncan Forbes of Culloden, it was
decided in 1743 to send the Black Watch to England.
The regiment was assembled at Perth in March of
that year, and it was explained to them there that they

were being sent to London so that they might show themselves to the King, who had never seen a Highland Regiment. Their departure was thus announced in *The Caledonian Mercury*: "On Wednesday last, Lord Sempill's regiment of Highlanders began their march for England, in order to be reviewed by his Majesty. They are certainly the finest regiment in the service, being tall, well-made men, and very stout." In a note to his *Sketches of the Highlanders*, General Stewart of Garth writes: "The King, having never seen a Highland soldier, expressed his desire to see one. Three privates, remarkable for their figure and good looks, were fixed upon and sent to London a short time before the regiment marched. These were Gregor M'Gregor, commonly called Gregor the Beautiful, John Campbell, son of Duncan Campbell of the family of Duneaves, Perthshire, and John Grant from Strathspey, of the family of Ballindalloch." Grant fell sick and died at Aberfeldy. The others "were presented by their Lieutenant-Colonel, Sir Robert Munro, to the King, and performed the broadsword exercise, and that of the Lochaber axe, or lance, before his Majesty, the Duke of Cumberland, Marshal Wade, and a number of general officers assembled for the purpose, in the Great Gallery of St James's. They displayed so much dexterity and skill in the management of their weapons, as to give perfect satisfaction to his Majesty. Each got a gratuity of one guinea, which they gave to the porter at the palace gate as they passed out. They thought that the King had mistaken their character and condition in their own country."

The regiment reached London at the end of April, and were reviewed at Finchley by Wade on 14th May. The soldiers were greatly annoyed by the fact that the King did not come to see them, and when they heard

that they were being sent abroad, mutiny broke out,
which resulted in the execution on Tower Hill of two
corporals and one private of the regiment. To show
the attitude of mind of Englishmen of that period to
Scotland, the following extract from a letter of Horace
Walpole to Sir Horace Mann, dated 19th May 1743,
is interesting:

"We are in more confusion than we care to own.
There lately came up a Highland regiment from
Scotland, to be sent abroad. One heard of nothing but
their good discipline and quiet disposition. When the
day came for their going to the water-side, an hundred
and nine of them mutinied, and marched away in a
body. They did not care to go where it would not be
equivocal for what King they fought. Three companies of dragoons are sent after them. If you happen
to hear of any rising don't be surprised—I shall not,
I assure you. Sir Robert Munroe, their lieutenant-
colonel, before their leaving Scotland, asked some of
the ministry, ' But suppose there should be any rebellion
in Scotland, what should we do for these eight hundred
men? ' It was answered, ' Why, there would be eight
hundred fewer rebels there.' "

In due course the regiment sailed for Flanders and
distinguished itself even in the eyes of the Duke of
Cumberland.

Wade proceeded to Flanders in 1744, where he
shared the command of the allied forces with the Duc
d'Aremberg (Austrians) and the Count of Nassau
(Dutch) against Marshal Saxe (French). Wade was
now over seventy years of age, was in failing health,
and this was his first experience of commanding an
army in the field. Like our leaders in the Crimea,
he found himself greatly handicapped by the divided
command, for d'Aremberg and Nassau made a point

of opposing any suggestions he put forward. They had no plans of their own, and the campaign opened with the allies having no line of action. The result was that Maurice de Saxe did what he liked with them, although the allies were much superior in numbers. Wade came in for much criticism at home, and his manœuvres were thus described in a London journal of the period:

"On the 30th July they encamped within four or five miles of Lille; on the 31st they lost a Scotch Volunteer before it. They looked also for a Field of Battle, but by great Providence no Enemy was nigh; on the 1st instant they were put in Fear, but as it happened danger was at a distance; on the 2nd they slept sound; on the 3rd the right wing foraged; on the 4th the whole army was reviewed; on the 5th they rested; on the 6th the right wing foraged; on the 7th did nothing; on the 8th received a Trumpet from Count Saxe about the exchange of prisoners; on the 9th sent him back again; on the 10th the Hanovarians foraged and had a gun fired at them from Lille; on the 11th the Britons foraged and had no gun fired at 'em, and the captain that was taken at Lille being exchanged, returned."

An officer of the Coldstream Guards wrote home thus: "The ability of M. de Saxe is such that he manœuvres our army as well as his own." Another young officer of the same regiment, in a letter home, says with considerable sarcasm: "I don't like all this moving about. I should not wonder if some day we were to fall in with the enemy."[1]

The French meantime reduced Courtrai, Menin, Ypres, Fort Knoque and Furnes. Wade did his best, but accomplished nothing. In addition to the trouble with his military colleagues, he had any amount of

[1] Quoted in Colonel Thornton's *Campaigners Grave and Gay*.

worries from home. He was ordered to adopt plans of campaign which were prepared in England by the Earl of Stair, who knew little or nothing about the situation. In a letter to Sir Horace Mann, dated 5th July 1744, Horace Walpole writes: " Our communication with the army is cut off through Flanders; and we are in great pain for Ostend; the fortifications are all out of repair. Upon Marshal Wade's reiterated remonstrances, we did cast thirty cannon and four mortars for it—and then the economic ministry would not send them. ' What? Fortify the Queen of Hungary's towns! There will be no end to that.' "

Wade's health completely broke down, and in October he applied for leave. He came home to England, and in March 1745 resigned his command, which was given to the Duke of Cumberland. The King, however, made Wade Commander-in-Chief in England, a position which he held until the Duke of Cumberland came home in December.

A most interesting account of this campaign from Wade's point of view is contained in a MS. entitled *An Authentick Narrative of the Campaign in Flanders of the Year 1744*, which is in the library of the Junior United Services Club, London. The handwriting may be Wade's, although there is no definite proof. Certainly the five articles, at the end of the account, in which charges against Wade are answered, are signed by Wade (initials) himself. Lord Harrington's letter to Wade accepting the latter's resignation, and dated from Whitehall, " March ye 18th, 1744," is as follows:

" SIR,

" I have laid before ye King what you represented to me concerning ye ill state of your health, & your Inability on that account to undertake ye

Command of his Majesty's Forces in the Netherlands for another Campaign, & have ye pleasure now to acquaint you, that his Majesty was pleased to express ye most perfect Satisfaction in your past Services, & at ye same time the greatest Regret upon finding you incapacitated by your Bodily Infirmities from continuing them in ye same Sphere of Action. & I am likewise directed to let you know, that ye King having appointed his Royal Highness ye Duke of Cumberland Captain Genl of his Majesty's Forces both abroad & at home; His Majesty is graciously pleased at your Request to dispence with your Service this Campaign, in the Command of his Forces in Flanders.

"I am with great Truth & Respect, Sir, Your Most Obedient Humble Servt,

" (*signed*) HARRINGTON."

In the rising of the Forty-five, Wade assembled an army at Newcastle. It consisted mainly of several regiments recalled from Flanders, and a number of Dutch troops, amounting in all to 10,000 men. The rest of the story is well known. Prince Charlie's army, instead of advancing to meet Wade after their victory at Prestonpans, marched on Carlisle, which they captured. Wade had been outmanœuvred, and the roads were so bad that after reaching Hexham, in an attempt to meet the Jacobite forces, he returned to Newcastle. By this time Cumberland was home from Flanders, and took command of another army of 8000 men. The story of the retreat from Derby need not be recapitulated here. Wade sent some of his cavalry to assist Cumberland in following up the Highlanders. Cumberland was appointed Commander-in-Chief of the whole British Army, and Wade retired. He was now seventy-three years of age.

Wade had once again been the subject of a verse. In a mongrel squib of the time, entitled *God Prosper our King*, Wade is given the honour of the following four lines:

" And, pray, who so fit to lead forth this parade,
  As the babe of Tangier, my old grandmother Wade?
  Whose cunning's so quick, but whose motion's so slow,
  That the rebels march'd on, while he stuck in the snow."

He made only one more public appearance, and that was as President of the Court Martial on Sir John Cope, which was taken publicly in the great room of the Horse Guards in 1746. Many memories must have come back to Wade as the evidence was given of that halt at Dalwhinnie and Cope's decision not to cross the Corrieyairack. Here is the finding of the Court Martial:

" The several examinations being finished all parties attending were dismissed. Whereupon we the said Field-Marshal, and other General officers before named, having duly weighed and considered the several matters laid before us, upon our examination into the conduct, behaviour and proceedings of Lieutenant-General Sir John Cope, Col. Peregrine Lascells, and Brigadier-General Thomas Fowke, contained in the foregoing state thereof, do, in further obedience to your Majesty's said Warrant, most humbly report that having made all the enquiries we could after proper persons who were able to give us any information relating to the matters aforesaid; and having examined all such as could be brought before us (there being several others whose duty on your Majesty's service in Scotland, would not admit of their leaving it to come before us) it doth appear to us, and we are unanimously of opinion that Sir John Cope made all the proper and necessary preparations for the support of his troops, with as much dispatch as he was able, both at Edinburgh and Stirling.

" That he also made the proper application to the chiefs of the clans that were reputed to be well affected to your Majesty and Government, for them to join your Majesty's troops.

" That he used all possible diligence and expedition before and in his march to Dalwhinny, considering the difficulties and disappointments he met with.

" That his attacking the rebels, on the Corriarrick, with any prospect of success, was impracticable.

" That his march to Inverness is justified by the unanimous opinion of the Council of War, and by the repeated assurances of being joined on the march and at Inverness, by the clans that were reputed to be well-affected to your Majesty and Government, of which he afterwards found himself disappointed, except by two hundred Munroes, who marched with him from Inverness to Aberdeen.

" That his going to Aberdeen, and then by sea to Dunbar, was the only proper measure he had left to take.

" That Sir John Cope's Disposition of his Body of Troops, in the Field of Action, was judicious; and the Ground on which they were engaged (according to the Plan and Description of many Officers who were present) appears to have been well chosen.

" That he did his Duty as an Officer, both before, at, and after the Action; and that his personal Behaviour was without Reproach.

" And that the Misfortune, on the Day of Action, was owing to the Shameful Behaviour of the Private

Men, and not to any Misconduct or Misbehaviour of Sir John Cope, or any of the Officers under his Command. . . .

" Upon the whole: We are unanimously of opinion that Sir John Cope's behaviour has been unblameable; and that there is no ground for Accusation against the said Sir John Cope, Colonel Peregrine Lascells, or Brigadier-General Thomas Fowke.

" All which is humbly submitted to your Majesty.

" GEORGE WADE.
" CADOGAN.
" JOHN FOLLIOT.
" RICHMOND.
" J. GUISE."

In his last years Wade lived in a Georgian brick house, which he built himself, in Southwood Lane, Highgate. Horace Walpole has a curious note about this house in a letter to George Montague in May 1778:

" I went yesterday to see Marshal Wade's house, which is selling by auction: it is worse contrived on the inside than is conceivable, all to humour the beauty of the front. My Lord Chesterfield said, that to be sure he could not live in it, but he intended to take the house over against it to look at it. It is literally true, that all the direction he gave my Lord Burlington was to have a place for a large cartoon of Rubens that he had bought in Flanders; but my lord found it necessary to have so many correspondent doors, that there was no room at last for the picture; and the Marshal was forced to sell the picture to my father: it is now at Houghton."

Walpole gives the following account of this picture, in his description of Houghton: " Meleager and Atalanta, a cartoon, by Rubens, larger than life;

brought out of Flanders by General Wade: it being designed for tapestry, all the weapons are in the left hand of the figure. For the story, see Ovid's *Metamorphoses*, lib. 3. When General Wade built his house in Burlington Garden, Lord Burlington gave the design for it."

Wade died on 14th March 1748, at the age of seventy-five. He was never married. *The Scots Magazine* of 1748 states:

"At London, aged 80,[1] George Wade, Esq., a Field-Marshal, Colonel of the third regiment of dragoon-guards, Lieutenant-General of the Ordnance, Member for Bath, and one of the privy council. His first commission bore date Dec. 26, 1690; whence he rose, under four succeeding princes, to the highest military honours. In 1704 he was made Adjutant-General, with a brevet of Colonel, by Lord Gallway. Five years after, he was honoured with a letter from the Emperor, and a commission of Major-General. In 1724 he was appointed Commander in chief in Scotland; and, while in that station, made the roads thro' the highlands. He commanded the allied army in the Netherlands in 1744, and the army in Yorkshire and Northumberland in the late rebellion. He died worth above 100,000*l*; 80,000*l* of which, he has left to two sons, officers in the army, and the remainder to two daughters."

These sons were named Captain William Wade and Captain John Wade. Wade also made provision in his will for the widow and children of his brother, William, who had been Canon of Windsor.

Marshal Wade was buried in Westminster Abbey, on the south side of the nave. Above a door from the south aisle to the cloisters there is a monument to him by Roubiliac.

[1] An error.

It is said that Roubiliac considered this monument his best work, and used to come and weep beneath it because it had been placed too high to be appreciated. This monument was erected in 1750. *The Scots Magazine* for August of that year describes it thus :

"Over the door leading to the cloysters in Westminster Abbey, an elegant monument, to the memory of Field-Marshal Wade, is lately finished by Mr Roubiliac. From the midst of a very curious pedestal, on which is affixed a medal, arises a Doric column of red marble, crowned with an urn. This column is adorned with a trophy composed of his ensigns of honour, arms, &c., which the figure of Time, placed on the left side, appears ready to destroy : but is repulsed by another figure on the right, which represents Fame. Several ornaments enrich the base, on which is the following inscription :

To the memory of
GEORGE WADE
Field-Marshal of his Majesty's forces,
Lieutenant-General of the Ordnance,
Colonel of his Majesty's third regiment of
dragoon guards,
Governor of Fort William, Fort Augustus and
Fort George,
And one of his Majesty's most Honourable privy council.
He died 14th March, 1748, aged 75."

CHAPTER XV

CONCLUSION

So ends this sketch of George Wade. It is extraordinary that so little record of him remains. It is even difficult in letters and memoirs of the period to discover any anecdotes about him. One is related by Sir Horace Walpole.

Writing again to Sir Horace Mann, on 10th January 1750, Walpole states:

"To make up for my long silence, and to make up a long letter, I will string another old story, which I have just heard, to this. General Wade was at a low gaming-house, and had a very fine snuff-box, which on a sudden he missed. Everybody denied having taken it: he insisted on searching the company: he did: there remained only one man, who stood behind him, but refused to be searched, unless the General would go into another room alone with him: there the man told him, that he was born a gentleman, was reduced, and lived by what little bets he could pick up there, and by fragments which the waiters sometimes gave him. 'At this moment I have half a fowl in my pocket; I was afraid of being exposed: here it is. Now, Sir, you may search me.' Wade was so struck that he gave the man a hundred pounds—and immediately the genius of generosity, whose province is almost a sinecure, was very glad of the opportunity of making him find his own snuff-box, or another very like it, in his own pocket again."

CONCLUSION

Wade cannot be numbered among our great soldiers or our great politicians.[1] He was probably too kindly a man to take his place with either class. He is, however, unique in that he was a man in a great position of whom no one spoke evil. He was given an ugly job to do in Scotland, yet he did it without offence. He enforced the Disarming Act, yet he incurred no ill-will. Even those men who had reason to dislike him and his works speak well of him. That his roads were for military purposes must be admitted. The strange thing is that the greatest military use that they were put to was by the armies of Prince Charles Edward Stuart. These troops used every inch of Wade's roads at one time or another during 1745–1746.

Wade was a man who made, and kept, many friends, who might so easily have been enemies. He was straightforward and honest, and made a point of seeing the other man's side of the question. The English part of him saw that he got his job done, the Irish part helped him to understand how he might be misunderstood by the Scottish Highlanders, and to do all in his power, by appreciating their point of view, to destroy that misunderstanding.

He was fond of the comradeship of wine, of the excitement of cards, of the company of women, of the comfort of good homes, good furniture, good appointments. He was somewhat conceited, loved to have his portrait painted, and enjoyed presenting these portraits to communities and individuals. He brought Van Diest from Holland to paint his portrait, and had him paint Colonel Gardiner and other officers at the same time. He presented at least one portrait of himself to Bath, and one to the laird of Ballindalloch. There is a

[1] Wade made one good speech in the House of Commons, in 1733, on the subject of courts martial.

picture of him as a young soldier in the National Gallery, and as an older one (by Hogarth) in the National Gallery of Ireland. In the Scottish National Portrait Gallery there is a painting and also a chalk-drawing of the Field-Marshal.

But his Highland roads are his best memorial. They may have been made for military purposes, but they were ways for light and learning—for folk moving out of the Highlands to learn about the world, for folk moving in from the world to learn about the Highlands. And now Wade's " new roads " are the " old roads," with ghosts on them and memories. Kindly ghosts indeed ! Worth while meeting, when your feet are tired of the very new road ! They hold now that romance which once they were held to have taken away. The new highway does the boasting—boasting, with its speed and its smoothness. But there is a call from the old " new roads." So this little book may help some folks to take the old road—and if they do, may they on some summer morning on the Corrieyairack see the ghostly soldiers feasting, may they meet a ghostly man of the Highland Companies among the rushes in Glen Cochill, and perhaps some night, as they come over from Trinafour, may they see a ghostly light in a ghostly Hutt at Dalnacardoch, and hear the ghostly voices of the first road-maker, Wade, and the last Jacobite, Struan, as they pledge each other in ghostly " bumpers."

APPENDIX

POST-WADE MILITARY ROAD-MAKING

THE following notes give a very brief summary of military road-making in Scotland after Wade's time.

Wade was succeeded in Scotland by General Clayton, and in 1741 and 1742 the latter made and repaired the road from Stirling to Crieff, with Caulfield as inspector. The latter constructed practically all the other military roads in Scotland, although there does not exist in the public phrase-book such a phrase as "a Caulfield Road." Caulfield spent something like £167,000 on new roads.

Cope had succeeded Clayton in 1743, and in 1744 he gave orders for the construction of a military road from Dumbarton to Inveraray. In 1745, Lascelles' Regiment was employed on this road, and moneys were granted for payment of workmen on this highway to Caulfield by Parliament during the years 1746-1748.[1]

But meanwhile a proper military survey of Scotland was being made, and by 1755 a map was produced. Many of the manuscript maps from which the complete map was made are in the British Museum. These maps are sometimes referred to as "Duke of Cumberland's Survey," and sometimes as "General Roy's Survey." They are scaled at two inches to the mile and show only roads and hills. No boundaries are given.

[1] For further details of Caulfield's work see Dr J. M. Bulloch's *Old Highland Highways*. Inverness, 1931.

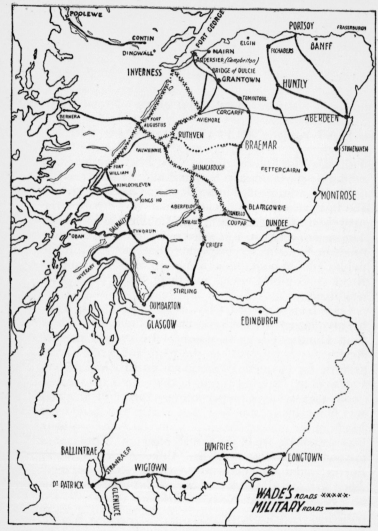

This map shows the lines of the military roads in Scotland. The road, which Wade planned, but which was not constructed, from Ruthven to Braemar is shown by a dotted line, while the road from the Corrieyairick by Glen Roy to Spean Bridge is omitted, as no information about it is available.

APPENDIX

Of course, there had been other than military road-making going on in Scotland for some considerable time. An Act of 1669 gave J.P.'s. power to demand six days' labour on the roads with a horse each year from all residents in a parish or county. At the same time proprietors made roads of their own. Then Parliament passed the Turnpike Act of 1751. This Act assessed farmers and proprietors in equal proportions for the maintenance of efficient public roads.

All this time military road-making was continuing, and by 1757 Caulfield had spent £130,000 on his roads. His Dumbarton to Inveraray road had been completed, Stirling had been joined to Fort William by Kingshouse, the Devil's Staircase and Kinlochleven, Tyndrum and Inveraray had been united, and a highway ran from Blairgowrie by Glenshee and Corgarff to the new Fort George, the building of which had been begun in 1749, but was not completed until 1763.

The military road-makers still went ahead. A great south highway from the bridge over the Sark to Port Patrick had been made, with a continuation to Ballantrae. In the far north Contin had been joined to Poolewe, Wade's north roads were connected from Dunkeld to Amulree through Strathbraan, and in the north-west several new highways had been constructed.

In 1767 Caulfield was succeeded by Lieutenant-Colonel Skene in the position of Inspector of Roads, and he took over some 858 miles of military highway and 139 miles of roads in course of construction. In an excellent article on the subject of the Military Roads published in the *Transactions of the Inverness Scientific Society and Field Club*, vol. v., Sir Kenneth S. Mackenzie,

Bart., gives the following summary of all the military roads made in Scotland:

	Miles
Wade's Roads [1]	258½
Fort Augustus to Bernera (Glenelg) .	43¼
Dunkeld to Amulree . . .	9½
Stirling to Fort William by Callander and Tyndrum	93
Stirling to Dumbarton . . .	34½
Dumbarton to Tyndrum . .	42
Tarbet to Inveraray and Tyndrum .	51
Dalmally to Pass of Brander . .	10
Fort George by Tomintoul, Corgarff and Braemar to Coupar-Angus .	111¼
Fochabers by Strathbogie and Cairn-mount to Fettercairn . . .	66
Strathbogie over Bin Hill to Aberdeen	36½
Stonehaven by Aberdeen to Portsoy and Fochabers	82½
Contin to Poolewe, Ross-shire . .	52
The Galloway Roads . . .	121

Later Roads—

	Miles
Loopline at Ballachulish to avoid Devil's Staircase . . .	28
Inverness to Fort George . .	12
Dulsie Bridge by Lochindorb to Aviemore	20
Aviemore to Grantown . . .	13½
Campbeltown to Nairn . . .	5
	78½
	1089½

With the advance and improvement of the turnpikes, the military upkeep of roads became less important

[1] See other list on page 110.

APPENDIX

and less necessary, and Lieutenant-General Mackay, Commanding the Forces in Scotland, wrote to the Lords of the Treasury, in September 1784, giving his views on the matter. He states that the military roads in Scotland amount to about 1100 miles, and continues:

"The first observation I would therefore make is, that however proper and necessary the making of these roads may originally have been, a line should be drawn where the country is capable of keeping them in repair by the Statute Labour, and where, from the wildness and barrenness of the country and the small number of inhabitants, the expense must unavoidably be defrayed by the public.

"To draw this line with care and propriety will require a more minute investigation than I have yet been able to make at large, but there are some which I am clearly of opinion may be now kept in repair by the country.

"The first I condescend upon is the line of road from the Bridge of Sark in Dumfriesshire to Port Patrick in Galloway, being 105 miles. To this road is joined a small branch from Ballintrae in Ayrshire to Stranraer in Galloway of 16 miles, which was begun some years ago by direction of Sir Adolphus Oughton, for the purpose of shortening the distance in the marching of troops from this country to Ireland by Port Patrick, which it does considerably. There are about five miles of this road, with some bridges, yet unmade. This the gentlemen of the country offer to complete for the sum of £800, and to keep up that road in the future without any expense to the public. I would therefore recommend the granting of this sum as it will be a saving of expense, and I am assured by the Inspector that the demand is very moderate.

"A considerable expense has been incurred for the

harbour of Port Patrick, which the Inspector informs me is now put in complete repair this season. I would therefore propose that the whole roads called the Galloway Roads should from this year cease to be a public charge.

"The only other line of road I would point out at present is from Stonehaven in Kincardineshire by Aberdeen to Portsoy and Fochabers in Banffshire, which, in my opinion, the country is well able to keep in repair, and, as I understand, has for the most part done so, though it still stands on the list of military roads. These are all I would immediately propose to cut off, but there are several other small branches which, I am clear, may, upon minute investigation, be so treated, at least by giving a small pecuniary aid to the country.

"I must observe to your Lordships that no regular system seems to have been laid down for the carrying on this business. The mode which has been adopted seems to me in many respects to be defective, and attended with unnecessary expenses. Some of these I shall point out, and shall likewise suggest in what manner I think they may be remedied.

"A number of horses have hitherto been bought and kept up constantly at the public expense, with carts, harness, and men to look after them, which, from the Inspector's accounts I have seen, make a heavy charge. I would therefore propose that the whole of these be sold off at the end of the year's work, to be accounted for, and that whatever horses and carts may be wanted in future, which should not be many, be hired by contract for the time of work allenarly. . . .

"I would further propose that, in so far as may be found practicable, the different roads should be kept in repair by contract, which would be attended by various advantages. The expenditure would be ascertained and all the contingencies cut off. The rebuilding and repairing of bridges that suffer by sudden torrents from the mountains is a large annual expense. This work has hitherto been plan'd out and executed by the best workmen the Inspector could find on the different lines of road, but who in many instances have acted very improperly. To remedy this I would propose that an overseer, properly qualified for directing this branch, be employed under the Inspector, which I am fully persuaded would prove a very material saving.

" I would likewise propose that your Lordships should give a fixed sum to the Inspector, in full as salary, travelling charges, clerk, stationery, and all demands whatever, to be paid by warrant from the Commander, in like manner as the other moneys issued to him.

" I think it proper to inform your Lordships that at present all the Highland roads are in general in very bad repair. This the Inspector owns to be the case, and says he found them so, and that it has not been in his power to remedy this, from want of troops to work upon them, with which I could not supply him from the small numbers we have had. This will prevent contracting till these roads are put in proper repair, after which I apprehend the charge will diminish considerably."

The repair of the Highland roads as a result of General Mackay's reports was mainly done by workmen employed at day's wages, and in 1789 the pay for military labour on roads had dropped to £142, 10s. 6d., and ten years later only 599 miles of military road were being kept in repair. In 1814 the Commissioners, appointed by the Road and Bridge Act of 1812, took over all the military roads and kept in repair only such as might be useful to the public.

In conclusion, let us take one glimpse of the soldiers working on the roads. It is given us by Dr Johnson. He was on the Bernera road when he met a party of soldiers at work and gave them some money. That night he put up at the inn at Anoch, and thus he writes:

" In the evening the soldiers, whom we had passed on the road, came to spend at our inn the little money that we had given them. They had the true military impatience of coin in their pockets, and had marched at least six miles to find the first place where liquor could be bought. Having never been before in a place so wild and unfrequented, I was glad of their arrival, because I knew that we had made them friends, and to gain still more of their goodwill, we went to them, where they were carousing in the barn, and added something to the former gift. All that we gave was not much, but it detained them in the barn, either merry or quarrelling, the whole night, and in the morning they went back to their work with great indignation at the bad qualities of whisky."

BOOKS ABOUT SCOTLAND

THE ELUSIVE RIVER

By GEORGE PRATT INSH

A roving survey of the Clyde from Daerhead to the Tail of the Bank.
Illustrated.   **6s.** *net*

LOVAT OF THE FORTY-FIVE

By W. C. MACKENZIE

The life of one of the most intriguing figures of Jacobite Romance—
Simon Fraser, Lord Lovat.

5s. *net*

LANDMARKS IN SCOTTISH LITERATURE

By GEORGE PRATT INSH

A history of Scottish literature from medieval times to the present day.

5s. *net*

SAINT ANDREW OF SCOTLAND

By Professor R. K. HANNAY

The story of Saint Andrew, the patron saint of Scotland, is told in this book
in a way that gives it interest to young and old alike.   How many Scots at
home and abroad know why Saint Andrew is their patron saint ?
Illustrated.   **2s. 6d.** *net*

IRREGULAR BORDER MARRIAGES

By "CLAVERHOUSE"

The romance of the runaway marriages on the Borders and the general interest
in the world-famous smithy at Gretna Green are amply proved by the number
of visitors to that spot each year.   The author has compiled a most interesting
history of the Gretna "priests" and their ceremonies around the historic anvil.
The book is illustrated with portraits of many of the old "priests," and other
unique pictures of great interest.

Illustrated.   **5s.** *net*

THE MORAY PRESS: Edinburgh & London

NEW NOVELS

BUNDLE AND GO
By G. and J. CUTHBERTSON
A stirring tale of the Jacobite Rising of 1715.　　**7/6**

∽

A RAGGED RENOWN
By OSWALD DALLAS
A story of the Thirty Years War.　　**7/6**

∽

THE BANDIT TRUST
By MILLIGAN WARRICK
A mystery tale by the author of "The Yawning Lion."　　**7/6**

∽

BID FOR FORTUNE
By J. S. FLETT
The adventures of four young men.　　**7/6**

∽

KINMONT WILLIE
By HALBERT J. BOYD
A romance of the Scottish Borders.　　**7/6**

∽

HAMISH
By J. J. BELL
A new character study by the author of *Wee Macgreegor*.　　**7/6**

THE MORAY PRESS: EDINBURGH & LONDON

The "Highlands & Islands" Series

SUN, CLOUD AND SNOW IN THE WESTERN HIGHLANDS: FROM GLENCOE TO ARDNAMURCHAN, MULL AND ARRAN. By ARTHUR GARDNER. With 116 Illustrations from the Author's Photographs. **12s. 6d.**

THE PEAKS, LOCHS AND COASTS OF THE WESTERN HIGHLANDS. By ARTHUR GARDNER. With 115 Illustrations from the Author's Photographs. **10s. 6d.**

THE FINDHORN: THE RIVER OF BEAUTY. By THOMAS HENDERSON. With 16 Illustrations from Pencil Drawings by JOHN CAMERON, and Map End-papers. **7s. 6d.**

THE ROAD TO THE ISLES: POETRY, LORE AND TRADITION OF THE HEBRIDES. By KENNETH MACLEOD. With an Introduction by MARJORY KENNEDY-FRASER. **7s. 6d.**

SHETLAND TRADITIONAL LORE. By JESSIE M. E. SAXBY. With Illustrations from Photographs. **6s.**

THE ROAD TO RANNOCH. By T. RATCLIFFE BARNETT. With 16 Illustrations from Photographs, and Map End-papers. **5s.**

AUTUMNS IN SKYE. By T. RATCLIFFE BARNETT. With 16 Illustrations from Photographs, and Map End-papers. **5s.**

THE LAND OF LOCHIEL. By T. RATCLIFFE BARNETT. With 20 Illustrations from Photographs, and Map End-papers. **5s.**

THE SECRET OF SPEY. By WENDY WOOD. With 28 Illustrations from Drawings by the Author, and Map End-papers. **5s.**

THE BEAUTIFUL ISLE OF MULL: WITH IONA AND THE ISLE OF SAINTS. By THOMAS HANNAN. With 16 Illustrations from Photographs by the Author, and Map End-papers. **5s.**

HIGHLANDS, HIGHWAYS AND HEROES. By D. C. CUTHBERTSON. With 31 Illustrations from Photographs, and Map End-papers. **5s.**

TRAMPING IN SKYE. By B. H. HUMBLE. With 15 Illustrations from Photographs, and 5 Maps. **5s.**

THE ROAD TO IONA: POETRY, LORE AND TRADITION. By KENNETH MACLEOD. **1s. 6d.**

THE MORAY PRESS: EDINBURGH & LONDON

MOUNTAIN DAYS IN THE ISLE OF SKYE

By

J. E. B. WRIGHT

Demy 8vo.   Cloth.   Illustrated.   12*s.* 6*d. net*

A real book for climbers and mountaineers.
The author is the founder of the "Lakeland
Mountain Guides," and was the first professional
guide in this country.   For the last ten years
he has been the head guide of the English
Lake District area.   He has made over 1200
ascents of different mountains in Central Europe
and the British Isles.   He has made over 2400
rock-climbing ascents in the Lake District.
North Wales, the Isle of Skye, Switzerland, the
Bavarian and Austrian Tyrol and the French
Alps.   Nearly 8000 mountaineers have engaged
his professional services.   His book is a record
of actual climbs in Skye, with ample details of
vital importance to mountaineers.   There are
over sixty pictures, reproduced from beautiful
photographs, and his narrative is interesting,
well-written and absorbing to all who have
made, or would like to make, the many ascents
with him.

THE MORAY PRESS: EDINBURGH & LONDON

AN
ANGLER IN ARCADIA

By

WILFRED WALTER MORRIS

Demy 8vo.   Cloth.   Illustrated.   *7s. 6d. net*

This is a book that will delight everyone who
has ever handled a fly-rod. The author takes
his readers through the Border country, and
tells of his fishing experiences on Tweed and
her sister streams, and of the people he has
met on the river banks. He leads them to
his favourite pools and streams, and weighs
the chances of Greenwell's Glory or Partridge
Spider against others on the casts, and while
his book is not a "practical guide," a great
deal can be learned about the fine art of
fly-fishing from his pleasant pages. It is a
charming book, written by a true disciple of
old Izaak, with a keen appreciation of nature.

THE MORAY PRESS: Edinburgh & London